Praise for

The Social Leader
and Frank Guglielmo & Sudhanshu Palsule

"Sudhanshu and Frank bring a fresh and much needed perspective to leadership in this great read. The book contains valuable insights and material for leaders navigating in our increasingly complex, interconnected world. I highly recommend that leaders and those of us in the business of getting leaders ready should read this book!"

—Mike Canning, CEO, Duke Corporate Education

"Farewell to lines and boxes, command and control, and other twentieth-century leadership and management practices. Social systems now rule the world...your employees, your customers, your associates, in short, everyone and everything is connected...socially. Learn to be a networked, community-focused leader from two of the best."

—Don E. Schultz, Professor Emeritus-in-Service,
Northwestern University, and president, Agora, Inc.

"Guglielmo and Palsule address the defining leadership challenges of our time: how do you lead when the organizational context is fundamentally communitarian? This insightful work is incredibly useful for leaders who find themselves straddling the disparate logics of the past with today's social world."

—Narayan Pant, the Raoul de Vitry d'Avaucourt
Chaired Professor of Leadership Development, INSEAD

"Can you be a leader in the future? Only if you change! In a world of ubiquitous connectivity, openness and access to information, and where society seeks greater engagement, leadership faces profound challenges and indeed, huge new opportunities. This work is not only timely but also critical for anyone in any leadership role in any group of people! Leadership will never be the same again!"

—Anton Musgrave, futurist and business strategist

"*The Social Leader* makes a compelling case for redefining how we think about leadership today. In an increasingly interconnected world, leadership requires building communities and unleashing the creativity and passion of those around you. The demand to lead with passion, purpose, and authenticity has never been greater."
—Andrea Jung, president and CEO of Grameen America, and former chairman and CEO of Avon Products

the SOCIAL LEADER

the SOCIAL LEADER

REDEFINING LEADERSHIP FOR
THE COMPLEX SOCIAL AGE

FRANK GUGLIELMO

SUDHANSHU PALSULE

First published by Bibliomotion, Inc.
39 Harvard Street
Brookline, MA 02445
Tel: 617-934-2427
www.bibliomotion.com

Printed in the United States of America

Library of Congress Cataloging-in-Publication Data

Guglielmo, Frank.
  The social leader : redefining leadership for the complex social age /
Frank Guglielmo and Sudhanshu Palsule.
      pages cm
  Summary: "The Social Leader structures a new approach to leadership and
provides tools for leaders to understand themselves in this new era of connectedness
and community"— Provided by publisher.
    ISBN 978-1-62956-015-1 (hardback) — ISBN 978-1-62956-016-8 (ebook) —
ISBN 978-1-62956-017-5 (enhanced ebook)
    1. Leadership.   2. Leadership–Social aspects.   I. Palsule, Sudhanshu.   II. Title.
  HD57.7.G84 2014
  658.4'092—dc23
                          2014018998

For Sil, who would much rather be in Philadelphia, and for Dee, who while never the Duke, was always a prince.

For Baba, whose kindness and wisdom inspires me each day, and for Daddy, whose presence is never far from me.

Contents

Contents

Acknowledgments

There are many brilliant, insightful people who have contributed to this book, and we would like to take a moment to acknowledge some of them. First and foremost, we would like to thank Sharon Grundfast. Sharon was responsible for bringing us together, and was the spark that led to this book. Sharon also coined the term, "Tenets of Social Leadership" to describe the thinking we were evolving. Over a couple of days in a sixteenth-century conference room at Trinity Hall, Cambridge and lunches at the Eagle Pub, the ideas began to take shape. We would also like to thank Don Schultz, who over many late night drinks and too many cookies, lent us his brilliant mind and ability to peer into the future to frame the implications of the Social Age.

No work stands alone. We have benefited from the work of the many great authors cited throughout the book. In addition we are grateful to the many individuals who have listened and added to our ideas along the way. Among these great contributors are: Mike Gissing, a long time thinking partner who generously read all of our first draft chapters adding his insights along the way, Michael Chavez, Mike Canning, Liz Mellon, Randy White, and Martin Asser at Duke CE, Lynn Ware, who saw the value of the ideas expressed here early on and provided constant encouragement and support, Schon Beechler for being a kindred spirit on the same journey, Rose Fass, who coined the term "new realities" and early on spoke of the sea change that is under way in the world, Anton Musgrave for the "future being here," Malcolm Goodale for helping to question the orthodoxies of leadership development, Narayan Pant for the Advanced Management Program at INSEAD, Pramod and Ram at the Indian School of Business, all the program directors and managers at Duke Corporate Education, and Pat, Monica, Joey, Fritz, and Robin for providing so many rich opportunities for working with many wonderful clients.

Acknowledgments

We've also had the benefit of learning from and observing many leaders who "get it" and are models of Social Leadership. Many of them have lent their stories to the pages of this book and include David Levin, Sally Shankland, Jonathan Donner, Angela Cretu, and Fabrizio Alcobe, among others.

We also thank the many participants of our leadership workshops across the world, who were both contributors to our research as well as for being the first leaders who heard our initial thinking on the subject.

The expression and dissemination of an idea, even in the world of social media, is greatly enhanced by the thoughtful guidance, editing, and curation of a top-tier publishing team. Erika Heilman, Jill Friedlander, Susan Lauzau, and Shevaun Beltzer at Bibliomotion have built a community of authors that adds immeasurably to the value of any one work's worth.

Finally and most importantly we thank our respective wives, Claudia and Saumya. Both brilliant professionals in fields removed from our own, they lent their time and insight to improve our thinking, provided incredible support for our efforts, and most critically, continue to tolerate us as husbands.

INTRODUCTION

The world we live in, work in, and lead in has not just changed in the last ten years—it has been replaced, period. This book is about remaining relevant as a leader given the new realities of the Social Age.

If Johannes Gutenberg's invention of the printing press in the mid-fifteenth century radically changed the way people gained access to information, Web 2.0 and the digitization of communication are overhauling the production and consumption of information on an unprecedented scale. We are witnessing nothing short of a revolution as global social networks, aided by rapidly falling costs of communication, reshape the way we create and sustain new social identities around common interests and shared passions.

Given the way social networks instantly transport information into the social domain, it is no longer far-fetched to imagine that very soon all information will be social. Instant, constant, ubiquitous, cheap, and unmoored from constraints of geography or time, information is being set free. The socialization of information is altering the very way in which we connect with one another. Not since the time we stopped moving around as nomadic hunters and took what was then the radically disruptive step of settling in one place has something so momentously changed the very grounds for our existence.

What this new information paradigm is doing is fundamentally shifting the way we relate to one another as human beings. We call this new reality "the Social Age," and it is characterized by three key points:

Introduction

1. The socialization of information
2. The rise of global, networked communities
3. The birth of the *prosumer*, who is completely at home in the Social Age

The term prosumer defines the shift in individuals from *con*sumers, who seek to acquire goods and services that are created for them, to contributors proactively engaged with companies and one another in the creation, development, and even the conception of the products and services they use.

Those of us who came of age before the Social Age are immigrants to it. We need to learn how to adapt and find ways of coping, perhaps even thriving, in this new world. Recently, it must have come as a sobering experience for immigrants to the Social Age to see that in a *Time* magazine /ABT SRBI poll in 2013 more than 70 percent of those between ages of eighteen and thirty-four regardless of political affiliation, thought that Edward Snowden had done a good thing by leaking NSA secrets.[1] After all, to digital natives what use is information if it is not put into the social domain?

So what is this Social Age that is emerging around us? In January 2014 the top fifteen social networking sites had 1.9 billion monthly visitors.[2] Social networks have an estimated quarter of a million new users creating online profiles each day.[3] From the GSM Association, an association of mobile operators and related companies, come these figures:

- More than 2.5 trillion text messages were sent in 2013
- More than 1000 users are signing up every minute of the day for mobile services that support media and learning
- 64 percent of mobile users live in emerging markets

The big shift taking place is that networked communities are fast becoming the dominant societal and organizational form, redefining how we work, how we interact, and how we lead others in our organizations.

While digital technology makes it possible to generate mass communication on an unprecedented scale, the entire communication network is actually run by individuals and groups whose membership is based on shared passion and interest. World of Warcraft has a million subscribers globally. Facebook's membership makes it the equivalent of the third-most-populated country in the world. Virtual communities based on the personal interests of members are constantly springing up. Communication is no longer what we thought it was: it is now about you, me, and all the others who share our passion.

One characteristic of social media is that the community of information sharers manages the way the network works. For example, the content on Wikipedia is monitored and managed by the user community. eBay works on the basis of community trust. Socially driven review sources such as Yelp for businesses and services, Rotten Tomatoes for films, Amazon reviews for books, and Glassdoor for employers are not only supplanting "expert opinions" but maintain quality by having their users review reviewers. Individuals rate and rank not only the content, but the quality of the reviews themselves. There is no "one" in charge, but the community has found a way to monitor itself, becoming a self-regulating organism. In the midst of all this, the following paradoxes of the Social Age are emerging:

1. We are spending an increasing amount of time online "alone," but are actually more connected to one another than ever before.
2. Digital technology apparently depersonalizes communication, but the nature of our passions and interests are driving the content and form of our communication.
3. We have become part of a droning 24-7 communication web, but our individual ideas and thoughts have reach on an unprecedented scale.
4. The world is becoming increasingly flattened through the globalizing force of digital communication, while the same technology is spawning new forms of cultural identities based on affiliation and identification.
5. As information becomes increasingly commoditized because of near-universal access, communities are beginning to surface around specific information areas.

These paradoxes play themselves out in the workplace as well. The interconnectedness of the Social Age and the ubiquitous availability of information are fundamentally altering the landscape in which we lead our organizations and our people. The structure of our companies, modeled after military hierarchies, was established to control the flow of information and the means of production. Today, these structures are giving way to flatter, more deeply connected community-based structures that work best when they harness the shared passions and interests of employees—what we call Social Energy, which we believe is fast becoming the differentiator for successful companies.

Moreover, the leaders who led like *generals,* directing and commanding the troops of our traditional organizations, are giving way to new leaders who are *mayors,* influencing diverse constituents and harnessing Social Energy to create success. The Social Age has moved us from a world where planning, forecasting, and strategy controlled business success to a world of complexity where unanticipated disruptive forces are common and awareness, agility, and proactivity in the face of ambiguity rule the day.

In this new world, given the new realities of the Social Age, are you leading in a way that is relevant? Have you dropped the command-and-control trappings of a general and found a way to bring together constituents across and beyond your formal sphere of responsibility to drive success? This book is intended to engage you in a conversation about just that, about becoming what we call a Social Leader.

THE PLAN OF THE BOOK

We have divided the book into two sections. Part 1 talks about the Social Age, its impact on companies and on leadership, and what you can do to shift your leadership approach to that of a Social Leader, making the transition from general to mayor.

Chapter 1 discusses the nature of the Social Age, the driving forces and defining features of this new reality. We look at the five core challenges of the Social Age and their implications for business and for leadership. Chapter 2 is about the business organization

Introduction

as a community. We explore the implications of the community metaphor for the way companies operate. We also look at how the shift to a community-based organization means understanding leaders as mayors who manage diverse constituencies. Chapter 3 refocuses on the five Tenets of Social Leadership and how these tenets interact to create authenticity in leadership. We demonstrate why it is more critical to focus on "who the leader *is*" rather than "what the leader *should do*." We also introduce you to the CAB model—conversations, actions, and behaviors—and examine the productive things leaders can do to succeed in the Social Age.

In chapter 4, "Understanding Yourself as a Social Leader," we will help you uncover your Personal Narrative and develop your Social Leader Learning Arc. The Learning Arc is an adaption of Joseph Campbell's hero's journey, and we will use it to help you create a model for learning from your experiences.

Chapter 5, "Becoming More: Developing Yourself as a Social Leader," builds the argument that leading by virtue of who you are is far more effective than chasing after competencies. Our emphasis is on expanding your productive leadership capabilities. Recognizing your blind spots and finding ways to compensate for them is more effective than attempting to turn weaknesses into mediocre capabilities.

Part 2 of the book looks at the Social Leader in action and examines each of the five leadership challenges of the Social Age, describing how the Tenets of Social Leadership help a leader succeed in addressing these challenges.

Chapter 6 is about leading from a state of mindfulness. In this chapter we describe why mindfulness is vital for anticipating discontinuity. Chapter 7, "Moving Through Ambiguity: Proactively Influencing the World Around You," talks about being an actor rather than a recipient and suggests ways of improving your personal agency by expanding your productive CABs in this area. Chapter 8, "Connected Constituencies: Relating to Others Authentically," addresses the challenge of creating influence given the din of competing viewpoints. Chapter 9, which focuses on adjusting perspective, discusses the challenge of social information and what it means to develop a learning mind-set. Finally, chapter 10 is about social scalability and how leaders must learn to adjust their approach for communicating with diverse constituencies simultaneously.

We will use two different sets of examples to illustrate concepts. First, we will look at actual examples of leaders drawn from research and from our own experience of working with several companies. We spent considerable time interviewing leaders at all levels to study the impact of Social Leadership and the shifting organizational context driven by the world of social media.

In part 2, in addition to stories from leaders in different companies, we will use a fictitious case study of a company called IKU Industries. We will introduce the company and follow it and some of its leaders. This case will help us examine the challenges of leading in the Social Age and the ways in which the tenets of Social Leadership can help executives meet these challenges.

Finally, within each of the chapters you will find opportunities and tools that invite you to pause, reflect, and look at yourself as a leader and at your organization as it operates in the Social Age. We encourage you to take the time to act on these opportunities, as your growth as a leader will occur only when you proactively examine your own lived experiences.

Part I

Making the Shift from General to Mayor

1

Leading in the Social Age

Lead from the back, and let others believe they are in the front.
NELSON MANDELA

In 1995, the commercial Internet came into existence and the world ended and was reborn. This is not an overly dramatic statement. If you are over thirty-five years of age, you learned to think and work in a world defined by planning for foreseeable trends and competitors. That world has been completely replaced by the Social Age—a time marked by digital connectivity, socially created information, and globally connected networks where constant disruption, agility, and competing points of view are the rule. If you are less than thirty-five years old, all you know is the Social Age. You joined the world of work in the twenty-first century and only know a world where the Internet and social media are part of life. You are native to this world and everyone else has immigrated to your world, bringing with them ways of thinking and leading that don't quite fit.

Let's take the example of Julia—a digital immigrant struggling to make the shift. Julia is the global head of strategy for a well-known telecom company in the United Kingdom. She is talented, in her forties, and has earned her place in senior management. With a track record of driving change in her past three organizations, she is now working in a corporate role. Many of the teams that report in to her are spread across the world and loosely linked together. Julia thought she knew all about managing a matrix and understood that she had to drive the corporate marketing vision and strategy across the regions and the local markets. She gathered her regional marketing heads at an off-site meeting to explain the company's new strategy to all of them and share the vision of the top team. She gave them lots of detail on how regions would provide information to the center, what the numbers were to look like, and, most importantly, the key processes that would make sure the matrix worked.

A year later Julia was starting to realize that she hadn't gotten the traction she wanted. In one particular region there was a young marketing head named Dmitri who had tweaked some of the core messages that came from her office and developed a marketing campaign using a local celebrity that clearly did not fit with the global marketing message. But the campaign was a big hit and the region was doing very well. Julia struggled with balancing the need for order and consistency with the corporate message and the need to manage employees like Dmitri. She congratulated him on the new campaign but asked him to henceforth report to her on every decision he made, and made it very clear that from now on, no campaign was to be launched without her approval. Dmitri soon left the company, and the numbers in the region began to dwindle. Before leaving the company Dmitri logged onto Glassdoor and made sure that he expressed his views on what was wrong with the organization.

Julia hadn't even heard of the "Glassdoor thing," as she called it when the head of HR brought it up at a Monday morning meeting. He connected to the website and displayed Dmitri's comment on the LED TV screen at the end of the room: "...good company to work for but there is zero culture of innovation. Managers like employees to do what they are told to do, and any attempt at thinking on their own or being creative is disallowed."

"But surely we have to enforce discipline and standard procedure across all regions!" exclaimed Julia when one of the meeting participants referred to the need to understand people like Dmitri. "We cannot be held ransom by anyone..." agreed Paul, the head of finance. Julia was struggling with the Social Age and she was playing by the book.

Julia saw in Dmitri an employee who was "refusing to play ball." If only she had been able to step into the shoes of a Social Leader, Julia would have found a way to reconcile Dmitri's passion for his market and his constituencies with the fact that a global strategy was essential to the company. Dilemmas such as these are exactly what complexity is all about. Rather than attempting to solve them in a linear, top-down fashion, Julia needed to explore complex solutions arising out of the conversations, actions, and behaviors characteristic of the Social Age.

Sally Shankland is the CEO of UBM Connect, one of the companies in UBM, a global marketing and events management company, and also heads the social and culture function for UBM Global. She has been working at UBM for twenty-five years, making her way up from an entry-level marketing role. Astute, authentic, and compassionate, Sally is the epitome of a leader who has made a successful transition into the Social Age. She talked to us about how, just fifteen years ago, she led differently and her need for control dictated how she ran meetings and teams: "I used to set very high standards for myself and for my team, and my natural style was all about 'lemme tell you how to do it.'" Calling this a default pattern for most leaders, she talked of how she had to make the shift from someone who led from the front to someone who knew how and when to get out of others' way. "For me," Sally said, "it used to be about giving my team the directions and saying this is where we've got to go . . . your job is to . . . and I would describe what I expected from them in detail. Then we met again in a week and I would ask them to report to me what they had done." As Sally said, "This definitely worked twenty years ago when business was not as frequently disrupted as now."

Sally told us of the shift she had to make in the way she led, and recalled the time UBM made the decision to move from its traditional print business to digital. Looking back, Sally remarked, "It wouldn't have worked to have taken that [top-down] approach" during that time of massive disruption in the business model. Sally talked about the way the disruption gave her the impetus to sit down with the team and start a conversation about a customer audience that was behaving very differently from the one UBM had traditionally served. "We sat down together and started mapping out the landscape, and over time questions began to emerge . . . How are people behaving? Why are they behaving that way? What is it that they need? What would it look like? What does the future vision look like?" It took time to reach a collective agreement, which, as Sally explained, was getting a group of diverse people to agree on what they were not going to do. Sally was guiding her team, not telling them what she wanted. She was facilitating the conversations and guiding the group to becoming a coherent whole. She was "leading from the back" rather than from the front.

Sally had a "beautiful moment" a year later when the team got together again. Sally said, her face lighting up as she recalled that moment of discovery, "I saw total alignment. We didn't have to ask if we were on the same page…we were like a school of fish that swam together making patterns."

When we spoke with Sally, she told us how the change in culture at UBM made Social Leadership possible. "UBM is now a business that is governed by principles rather than by rules," she said. Speaking about the positive impact that the paradigm shift created, Sally talked of how that made it possible for leaders to adjust: "We learned how creating value is more important than capturing value…and in the end, when we have created value, we end up capturing value anyway, but that is not the purpose." That is an apt descriptor for the Social Age: the only way we can capture value is when we don't try to capture value, but rather work toward creating value for our networks in the community.

The Social Age is a new order brought about by the confluence of three major forces: digital technology, globalization, and changing mind-sets and attitudes. Together, these forces are creating profound changes in the world and, more specifically, in the environment in which we work and lead. Julia's story is about one of the ramifications of this Social Age. She was left facing the unplanned consequences of actions that had made perfect sense in previous years but were no longer useful in the current context. Julia needed to understand that, to lead in a rapidly changing Social Age, she had to tap into the passion that drives people in differing constituencies and harness them to a common purpose. What Julia needed to do was step into the shoes of a Social Leader, just as Sally did.

The Social Leader is a phenomenon whose time has come. We define the Social Leader as one who is able to harness the passions of networks of individuals by generating the Social Energy needed to achieve a common purpose. Let's begin our journey into what it means to be a Social Leader by looking at some of the characteristics and challenges of the Social Age.

WHAT IS DRIVING SOCIAL LEADERSHIP?

The Social Age is here. It is present and will be the context in which you lead from today onward. Let's take a moment to step back and identify the key characteristics of this new reality.

The Social Age is characterized by:

1. Socially created information. The lines between public and private spaces are becoming increasingly blurred, leading to an overlapping social space. Information is therefore finding itself increasingly in the social space, created continually and communally and accessible to all through technology. Our organizations are becoming increasingly inhabited by individuals, and under scrutiny from stakeholders and customers, who possess three resources on a scale that is unprecedented: ubiquitous access to social information; an expectation that they can engage anyone and everyone in conversation to shape the point of view of the community; and speedy, cheap communication that allows them to react to events in real time.

2. The rise of global, networked communities. Driven by passion and purpose, groups of people from around the world are becoming linked together in communities that are dramatically transforming the way we communicate, make choices, take decisions, and engage with one another. These global communities are also sharing information and becoming points of influence in novel ways. With information fast becoming a commodity, the competitive landscape is dramatically shifting to a context in which it is the social relevance of information, rather than the information itself, that is a source of advantage. The problem with social relevance is that we are no longer in control of it; rather, socially networked communities whose actions, decisions, and interactions are beyond our jurisdiction bestow relevance upon information.

3. The birth of the prosumer, who is completely at home in the Social Age. The term prosumer defines the shift in individuals from consumers, who seek to acquire goods and services that are created for them, to contributors proactively engaged with companies and one another in the creation, development, and even the conception of the products and services they use. A mind-set of transparency, participation, and engagement have created a new generation that is starting to have an impact on the creation, dissemination, and absorption of information. As employees and as consumers, they expect to have a voice in the products and strategies of companies they care about.

As a result of these three factors, our organizations are being driven to act more like communities than like traditional hierarchies. Leaders in organizations are experiencing a shift from planning to agility; instead of generals directing their troops, they are becoming mayors managing diverse constituents. All in all, these factors have created five leadership challenges that are unique to the Social Age:

1. Dealing with discontinuity. Although business discontinuity has always been around, it occurred in rare and dramatic ways. Today, business discontinuities are the norm—from mobile apps transforming the cell phone to streaming video destroying the video rental market to data mining of search terms remaking epidemiology.

The ability to pick up "weak signals" emerging from an adjacent technological or industry space and respond to them speedily is fast becoming a leadership challenge of huge importance. When Nokia was at its pinnacle of success in the early years of this century, it failed to capitalize on a few weak signals that were happening outside its field of vision. The most critical one was Google, a search engine company, buying a small start-up in Silicon Valley called Android in 2005. As this was happening in an adjacent space, it ostensibly had nothing to do with the world of cell phones and telecommunication.

But by 2008, Android had emerged as a serious contender to Nokia's own operating system, Symbian, and Nokia's mobile phone business entered a downward spiral from which it never recovered.

2. Moving through ambiguity. Leaders are under pressure to act in a constant state of ambiguity, and must trade predictability for confidence in their ability to be agile despite frequent disruption. For example, no longer is it possible for a leader to focus only on "her team" or "his organization." Leaders today are expected to influence a wide range of constituencies, sometimes two or three steps removed from their "official" range of responsibility. These relationships are often devoid of authority or loyalty, making them complex to manage. The emergence of networked groups of constituents tied together by shared passion and common interests has created more complex business landscapes than ever before. Further, the need to influence multiple stakeholders who may not be in agreement with you is another major shift from the traditional model, in which old factors of loyalty and reporting lines made it easier to "manage" people.

3. Demands of connected constituencies. The socially enabled organizations in which we lead are driven by the demands for transparency from our instantly connected constituents. In fact, transparency is fast becoming the defining characteristic of the Social Age thanks to the blurring of lines between the private and public spheres. In the Social Age, it is no longer possible for a leader to have a "game face," one that is shown to the world but is inauthentic. In fact, we are finding that the demand for authenticity has never been higher, as workplaces become increasingly flattened and transparent, and a new generation of "digital natives" and early converts to the Social Age start exercising their demands for transparency.

4. Working with social information. The speed of change and the rapid propagation of information mean that the Social Leader must be able to operate using multiple perspectives. Constituents' expectations for multi-way communication and constant commentary result in "meaning" being created in public continually, communally, and quickly—i.e., social information. The ability to make adjustments and remain adaptive, to work with contradictions, and to do all this without compromising credibility have become essential aspects of leadership in the Social Age.

5. When everyone has a megaphone. The inhabitants of the Social Age carry megaphones and live life out loud. Speaking to the entire organization was once the purview of senior leaders. Thanks to social media—from purely social sites such as Facebook to proprietary internal social media platforms, to socially driven work platforms to external blogs devoted to a company or industry—everyone who cares about a company can speak to everyone else who cares, inside an organization or outside it. In this new reality, a leader must be able to pitch communications in a way that is appropriate for an individual, a group, and the community all at once. As importantly, a leader needs to be aware of how communication travels like a light wave, spreading across communities within a network in real time.

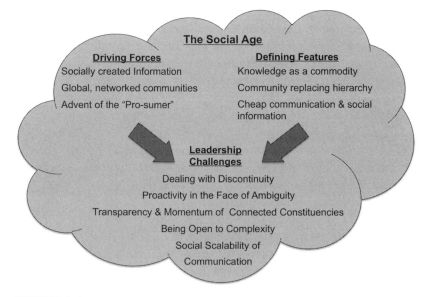

FIGURE 1-1   The Social Age

STAYING RELEVANT IN THE SOCIAL AGE

It was almost twenty-five years ago that John Kotter wrote the deeply influential *Harvard Business Review* article "What Leaders Really Do."[1] He told us that a leader's primary role is to help people cope with change and that leaders actually do three things: they set direction, align people, and motivate and inspire others. That article set the focus of leadership for an entire generation, and corporate training departments, business schools, and individual executives all took this sound advice to heart. These efforts set in motion a school of thought that placed leaders at the pinnacle of sense making within organizations. They became accountable for creating meaning and bringing employees together in common cause. Around the same time, something else of consequence happened: the Internet came into being and forever changed the world.[2]

The birth of the information age and the so-called knowledge era provided us with access to huge amounts of information, and before we knew it, information was fast becoming a commodity. Information was no longer at a premium, dealing the first blow to hierarchies sustained by the notion that those at the top knew more than the rest. Soon, the information age gave way to the Social Age, a post-information age in which *information*—facts and data plus a point of view—is created continually, communally, and simultaneously by networks of people joined by shared passion around a topic rather than through geographical or organizational allegiance. We've turned from mere consumers of information into consumers *and* producers.

The year 2013 will be remembered for two events that marked the passing of the old world order: one, the *Encyclopedia Britannica* ceased publication. What was once considered the pinnacle of objective knowledge—gleaned and documented by experts—was replaced by Wikipedia, a platform on which information could be published and edited by anyone with Internet access. Two, Google celebrated its fifteenth birthday, a coming of age of the divide separating those born before Google and those who have only ever worked, learned, and communicated in a world where information is fully available and social media communication is the norm. In two swift blows, the world was transformed in ways far more impactful than those wrought by Gutenberg's fifteenth-century invention of the printing press.

So, coming back to where we began, are you leading in a way that is relevant to the digitally connected community? The role of leadership in helping an organization cope with change and uncertainty has perhaps never been more important. The tasks of leadership that Kotter outlined—alignment, direction, and inspiration—appear as valid as ever. *How* a leader delivers in a hyperconnected world where employees have access not only to facts and data but to everyone's viewpoints is what has changed dramatically. One need only look at the results of the 2013 Edelman Trust Barometer[3] and note that 40 percent of people who consider themselves "informed" about a company find the statements of a CEO credible while 41 percent find what they learn through social media credible. Clearly, leaders are now competing with "the community" over who gets to make sense of what is happening in and to the organization.

But Social Leadership is not about competing with "the community" to create a galvanizing point of view. Rather, it is about how to lead in a Social Age that has been reshaped by digital media and in organizations that have become socially enabled with employees more connected than ever before.

The growth in worldwide connectivity over the last twenty-five years has been astounding. According to the Internet Systems Consortium the number of Internet hosts has grown from just over 300,000 in 1990 to well over 900 *million* in 2012.[4] Facebook announced in its 2013 Q1 financial filings that it has 1.11 billion members. It has grown so large that, if it were a country, it would now rank third in terms of population, ready to surpass India for the number-two spot very soon. A 2012 study in the United States found that 75 percent of employees check some form of social media at work regularly[5] while a study in Ireland found that the rate was 80 percent.[6]

Virtual communities based on personal interests spring up constantly. Digital innovations now connect us personally and in real time to events, items of personal interest, and content that sparks our passion. This digital coming together involves not just a person and information of interest to her, but a person, information of interest, *and* other people who find the information of interest. Today, connections have become instant, constant, and unmoored from constraints of geography or time. Talent is more mobile than ever. In such a world, the ability to harness the passions, interests, and relationships among people is fast becoming a key differentiator of successful leadership.

OUR MILITARY HERITAGE

Those of us who came of age before this new socially connected digital world are immigrants to it, and we need to learn how to succeed in this new context. From the dawn of the Industrial Revolution, the root metaphor around which organizations have traditionally been led, either consciously or inadvertently, has been military. "Marshal your troops" and "Get back to the war room" continue to be common phrases used in business; in an organization that one of us was connected to, common cautions were, "Don't raise your head above the parapet" and "Watch out for the snipers." We talk of "providing air cover" and "watching your back," little realizing how deeply pervasive the military metaphor has been. The keys on our computers echo the same message: the Esc key, the Ctrl key, the Cmd key all resonate with the metaphor. So do the origins and the context of the word "strategy," which embodies the worldview of top military brass planning an invasion, then communicating it through the ranks and finally to the troops, who then have to follow the orders. As parents of children who have grown up embracing a Social Age in which transparency and constant availability of information are taken for granted, we are concerned that the military metaphor has outlived its usefulness, even as many organizations continue to flog it.

One big reason that the military metaphor worked for organizations was that the world in which we have been operating was relatively stable and followed a linear order of causality and predictability. Leaders as "generals" led their troops to war, and that model worked as long as the enemy could be identified and strategies could be developed that relied on a predictable macro environment.

COMPLEXITY VERSUS LINEARITY

Complexity is the opposite of linearity, not the opposite of simplicity, a common misunderstanding. It happens when unforeseeable factors converge and interact in unpredictable ways to create a situation that is not only unpredictable but immune to the traditional rules of decision making. Complexity has three main characteristics: one, a complex system is self-organizing, which means that it consists of agents whose actions cannot be controlled or predicted; two, it is adaptive, which means that the diverse agents make decisions to interact with one another; and three, it is emergent, meaning that the result will always be greater than the sum of its parts. In a nutshell, complexity is the absence of the traditional data points and information that we rely upon to make decisions when leading like generals.

It shouldn't take long to note two things: one, complexity is increasingly defining our business landscape. In a study we conducted with senior decision makers and CEOs in twenty-four different organizations, including the United Nations, spread across a number of industries, 89 percent of the over 500 interviewees agreed that complexity (defined by the pace of change and the unpredictability of the system) is their number-one challenge. Two, in a complex business landscape defined by self-organization, adaptability, and emergence, the root metaphor of leadership as a general commanding his troops is seriously limited.

So what is the alternative to the military metaphor and to the notion of the leader as general? We are convinced that the root metaphor for organizations in the Social Age has already shifted to community. Studying successful leaders tells us that the apt metaphor for the Social Leader is that of a mayor.

RETHINKING LEADERSHIP FOR THE SOCIAL AGE

A business with leaders operating as mayors, employees as members of networked communities, and teams held together by common passions and interests rather than hierarchy is not only possible but a requisite for meeting the core challenges of today's business environment.

What does it mean to lead in this new Social Age? The topic of leadership has been explored and analyzed by psychologists, business experts and laypeople for years; some have looked for timeless principles and have made great strides in understanding the underlying aspects of successful leadership. Others have looked for specific behavior patterns and have provided prescriptive models of successful leadership actions often targeted at specific types of followers, leaders, or organizations. But nearly all those who have sought to understand leadership have agreed on one thing: leadership does not occur in a vacuum. Leadership occurs between the leader and the led within the context of the world they inhabit.[7]

Our own understanding of leadership proceeds from two core beliefs. First, the proper context in which to understand leadership is the moment in history in which it occurs. This transcends particular organizations, particular types of employees, and particular cultures. All of these are important, but "the times" in which the leader seeks to lead, we believe, profoundly influence what it takes to become a successful leader. For example, in *Personal Growth, African Style*[8] one of the authors describes the challenges of leading in post-apartheid South Africa, as the African empowerment movement advances into a second generation. Much of the learning and guidance on leadership in that work is based on the deep influence of the particular moment in history in which South Africa finds itself.

In this book we seek to understand leadership in the current historical moment of the Social Age, a time when the digital world has expanded our capacity for social networking in the "real world" and has rekindled the age of operating in communities.

Our second core belief is that leadership must be understood at the level of the individual leader—who he or she actually is. This means understanding the fundamental aspects of successful leadership in this moment in history and helping individuals expand these characteristics within themselves.

In this regard, we find ourselves taking a different approach from those authors and leadership development practitioners who advocate the idea of leadership *competencies*. Leadership competencies are often described as patterns of behavior, and it is quite popular in leadership development practice to seek to identify a set of leadership competencies tied to a particular organization and then help leaders either acquire or improve these patterns of behavior.

Embedded in competency approaches to leadership is the assumption that the proper focus for improving an individual's capacity to lead is based on changing or redirecting his behavior. An individual's behavior is unquestionably a crucial component of his ability to lead. However, we think that helping a person acquire a new pattern of behavior that is inconsistent with who she is as a person is not a recipe for either long-term success or personal fulfillment. Rather, we believe that helping an individual increase her success at leading depends on helping her to better understand who she is and how she can capitalize on the most productive aspects of her own approach. Our research indicates that authenticity is crucial when operating in an interconnected world in which organizations function like communities. Therefore, helping individual leaders to grow "who they are" needs to become the primary goal of leadership development. This is in contrast to the more common approach of looking at leaders' behavior in terms of competencies and helping them change "what they do."

THE TENETS OF SOCIAL LEADERSHIP

While we will explore the concept of the Social Leader fully throughout the book, we start by proposing the Social Leader framework based on what we refer to as the Tenets of Social Leadership. We have developed these tenets after carefully examining the hundred-odd years of research on the topic of leadership and applying our combined experience of close to sixty years helping develop leaders.

> *Mindfulness:* the capability to maintain and act on four types of awareness: temporal, situational, peripheral, and self
>
> *Proactivity:* the belief that one is in control of one's own actions and seeing oneself as able to influence events rather than being dragged along by them

Authenticity: engendering in others a belief in your own credibility; the ability to build personal trust in a relationship and positively confront disagreement and competing points of view

Openness: the capacity to act, thrive, and learn from situations that are complex, novel, and ambiguous

Social scalability: fluidly communicating separately and jointly to: one individual, a small group, and the entire organization

We intend to look at the productive and unproductive aspects of these tenets as they relate to an individual's success at being a Social Leader and address the five core challenges of leading in the Social Age.

Social scalability is a new concept that we believe is crucial to leading in a community-based organizational context. Social scalability is the leader's capacity and comfort in moving between leadership situations of different scale—leading one person, a small group, or a large organization. One of the greatest changes brought on by social connectivity is the closing of the social space between leaders and followers. A leader's success today will in large part be based on her capacity to move fluidly between leadership moments, and these moments will involve groups of different sizes—often outside the leader's control or choosing.

IN SUMMARY

The Social Age is characterized largely by three key points: 1) socially created information, 2) the rise of globally connected communities, and 3) the birth of the prosumer who is completely at home in the Social Age. These forces have defined the Social Age as a time where knowledge is a commodity, the community is replacing the hierarchy as the basic structure of work, and cheap communication and social information impact everything.

Together, these aspects of the Social Age have created five crucial leadership challenges:

- Discontinuity
- Ambiguity

- Connected Constituencies
- Social Information
- Everyone having a megaphone

To deal with these challenges leaders need to evolve their mindsets, approaching leadership as if they are mayors harnessing the Social Energy of diverse communities rather than generals leading troops into battle. We believe that this is best done through a focus on the five Tenets of Social Leadership:

- Mindfulness
- Proactivity
- Authenticity
- Openness
- Social Scalability

2

The Business Organization
as a Community

Our business has always been about community.
DAVID LEVIN, CEO of McGraw Hill Education
and former CEO of UBM

UBM plc is a global media company that delivers in-person events, online publishing, and print programming. Companies like UBM felt the tremors of changes in the environment earlier than those in other industries. The Social Age was dawning fast as the changing environment impacted the media business like no other. Information, the lifeblood of UBM's business, was rapidly turning into a commodity. The world was moving online and UBM was stuck in the "inky" world, which meant that it needed nothing short of a transformation.

The technological changes that were happening had a huge impact on UBM's business model. Classic economies of scale were appearing as platform economies in software. Globalization and interconnections meant that supply chains were getting "mashed up." As David Levin, the former CEO who led the transformation of UBM, says, "the relentless pressure of a 24-7 continual bombardment was happening at a pace that was unprecedented." In an interview with the *Daily Telegraph* in early 2012 referring to print journalism, David commented, "software has eaten the business." What David and his team had to confront was the fact that the plummeting cost of technology and mobility was profoundly changing the way we work and connect with one another.

When David took over as CEO of UBM in 2005, the business had a great balance sheet but was in terrible strategic shape. More than half the business centered on controlled circulation ad-driven magazines, and the world was rapidly going online. Furthermore, the business had a tiny footprint in the emerging markets, though a significant presence in the UK and Europe. David talks of having to make sure that his team was not in denial, as that was very much part of the earlier culture. "I had to bring the Grim Reaper into the room," David says. He taught the others to stop pretending that all was well before it was too late. "Death is a part of life—don't fear it" was David's message. "I had to get them to acknowledge that things are born and things die, and that there was nothing wrong with it; it's a natural cycle of life." And then he adds, "but I also had to talk to them about hope. And passion. The nature of transformation is that you have to do both things at the same time; while you talk of some things dying you also have to give them hope about the other things. That is what transformation is all about."

What marks David's story and the UBM story as noteworthy is the way in which the transformation happened. He helped his team transform their collective mind-set: from managing a set of UBM companies to building a UBM business community. When we spoke to Ted Hopton, the community manager at UBM, and asked him to define what UBM meant by "community," his answer was revealing: "The UBM community is an online community with our clients, customers, and our own people: it is one unbroken unit. But most importantly, the online community is a reflection of our internal culture."

As we look at the challenges that faced UBM we see those that are common to the Social Age: significant business disruption; the need to be proactive amid chaos and ambiguity; the pressure to remain true to core values while transforming the business (authenticity); taking in new information and new perspectives; and the challenge of connecting with and speaking simultaneously to all of their people and constituencies, individually and collectively.

UBM's solution to these challenges was to change the fundamental premise of the organization—away from hierarchical divisions and toward a community. But first they had to sell almost half the business, "and that was a command decision" as David said. UBM did more than a hundred acquisitions and fundamentally transformed itself as a business. Having done that, David assumed his role as a mayor, building connections across various constituencies within the business, helping everyone come to terms with a new set of realities and building the infrastructure that allowed everyone in the community to have a voice and contribute.

Step back a moment from UBM and look at your own business. Imagine you have some of the best people working for you. You have put in place all of the "people processes" that current management science tells you are important—development programs, upward feedback, performance-based compensation systems, and a company mission. But you keep asking yourself, "Why are no new ideas hitting my desk?" and "Why does every new challenge not elicit ten highly charged individuals who have a new way to solve the problem?" and "Why doesn't every opportunity bring a flood of proposals from my people?" It may well be that the very design of your organization and the underlying model you have based your structure on (consciously or not) are not set up to unleash the full potential of your people. Maybe the model worked at an earlier time in an environment less complex. We think it is time to start making the shift from bureaucracy to community.

The reason business organizations exist is that they solve problems inherent in delivering the goods or services the business seeks to deliver. For nearly 150 years the core problem common to all businesses was the need to organize activity and control both intellectual capital and the means of production. As we saw in the previous chapter, the Social Age has radically shifted organizational focus to three crucial points:

1. The socialization of information
2. The rise of global, networked communities
3. The birth of the prosumer

What is the core challenge for business organizations that want to be successful in the Social Age, where disruption is business as usual and complexity is the name of the game? It is to create and retain social significance by developing a constant flow of value for customers and stakeholders. But in an age where employee loyalty and longevity, clear-cut vertical reporting lines, and a relatively stable environment can no longer be depended upon, the only way organizations can create social significance is by drawing upon purpose. For a business to stay agile and quickly respond to disruptions in the environment, the core capabilities must shift from organization, communication, and control—the key contributions of a bureaucracy—to empowerment, enablement, and harnessing of passion, the cornerstones of purpose.

FROM HIERARCHY TO PURPOSE: THE STORY OF VISA

For Dee Hock, the founder of Visa, the Industrial Age embodied the bureaucratic and command-and-control institutions that, over the past two hundred and fifty years, grew to dominate our commercial and social lives. In Hock's opinion, "These institutions are becoming increasingly irrelevant in the face of complexity. They are failing not only in the sense of collapse but in the more common and pernicious form of failure—inability to achieve the purpose for which they were created."[1] Dee Hock based his vision for Visa on the philosophy of interconnectedness and community. In his words, "The whole thing behind the creation of Visa has not been about banks or merchants or credit or cardholders. It was about connections…it was about relationships and growth; about all things growing from one another, and everything growing from some indefinable essence that is about all things being inseparably interrelated."

Hock was at least thirty years ahead of his time in creating an organization based upon the salient principles of business as a community. Today Visa holds almost 40 percent of market share, its products are created by twenty-two thousand owners—member financial institutions—and accepted at more than thirty million merchant locations in more than two hundred countries. The company processes more than sixty billion transactions, producing an annual income of $4.4 trillion—the largest single block of consumer purchasing power in the global economy.

Visa began as and continues to be a community. Hock's words ring true when he writes: "All institutions are no more than a mental construct to which people are drawn in pursuit of a common purpose: a conceptual embodiment of a very old, very powerful idea called community." Some of the organizational principles upon which Visa was founded come very close to what we will describe in the next section as the building blocks of a business community. They are:

1. Power, function, and resources should be distributed to the maximum
2. Authority should be equitable and distributive
3. To the maximum degree possible, everything should be voluntary
4. Leaders should induce, not compel change
5. Organization structure should be infinitely malleable yet extremely durable

What Hock did was to create a purposeful organization that was able to draw upon and harness the passion of its people, who were linked together with one common purpose. As we shall see, while times have changed and the world is a very different place than it was thirty years ago, purpose continues to be a dominant principle in building a business community.

FROM TRADITIONAL ORGANIZATION TO BUSINESS COMMUNITY

The traditional bureaucratic organization has been enormously successful for over a hundred years. But, to paraphrase Dee Hock's question, is it still achieving the purpose for which it was created? Even more important, is that purpose still relevant? There are already signs that the ways in which people organize to meet the present-day challenges of work must evolve.

The following diagram demonstrates how, over time, the most optimal model of organizing the business enterprise has evolved, and with it the degree of centralization that has driven its success. Both the guild and the traditional organization succeeded in their time

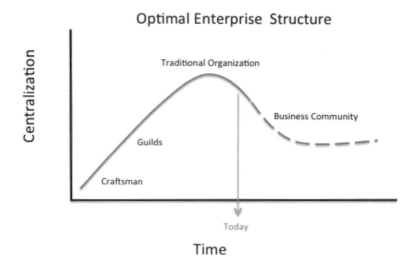

FIGURE 2-1. Optimal Organization Structure

because the organizational structures that emerged from these models helped master the most pressing challenges of the time: control of professional standards and protection of intellectual property. The key organizational challenge at the time of the guilds was controlling "know-how," because it allowed the guild to manage competition and the quality of goods and services. This was possible because business environments were generally self-contained and there was very little (by today's standards) knowledge sharing across different business environments. In this context, know-how was controllable and the guild was the vehicle through which the "secrets" of a profession passed on to the tightly controlled membership of that guild.

Over time, financial capital in the form of cash and the means of production—machinery, processes, etc.—became the primary resources to be controlled, and were much more important than know-how. Know-how either became widely available through education or was built into business processes. The ability to produce complex products in large volumes to satisfy ever-widening markets became the primary challenges of a business. Traditional organiza-

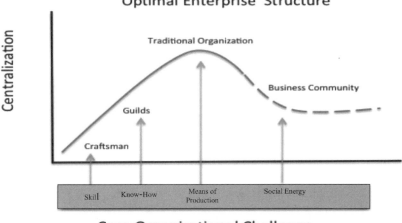

FIGURE 2-2 Core Organization Challenges

tions, with the division of labor and structured control over processes as their core capability, were perfectly suited to these conditions.

The vast majority of business organizations today are structured along this traditional model. But the cracks are starting to show. In a 2013 Duke Corporate Education CEO study,[2] what emerged was that the context in which CEOs were being challenged was dictated by two irrevocable facts: challenges are less predictable and knowledge is less reliable. The core capability of know-how and means of production are suddenly becoming less relevant to the ongoing success of a business enterprise. What is going to replace know-how and means of production are purpose and passion—what we call Social Energy.

For a Social Leader, the culture of the business is the environment that must be shaped. The Social Leader is deeply aware that the only way to effectively lead an organization in the Social Age is to create a culture that:

- Supports its people, enables them to give their best, and provides them with space for creativity

- Engenders Social Energy by generating passion and a sense of common purpose
- Is adaptive to the external environment, picking up the weak signals that emerge from the periphery and generating value in partnership with the environment

While business success has always depended on the business's ability to promote an engaging culture and be in touch with its environment, in the Social Age it is no longer an option. It is the only way that companies can remain agile and responsive to the disruptions in the environment. It is also the only way to deal with complexity.

THE UBM JOURNEY TO COMMUNITY

The London UBM offices are at Blackfriars, in the southwest of the city, adjacent to the old Blackfriars Bridge that leads to St. Paul's Cathedral. Not far from the UBM office is the site where Shakespeare's Globe Theatre was built in the year 1599. Not a bad setting for then-CEO of UBM, David Levin, whose favorite course during his MBA at Stanford was drama.

David took over as CEO of United Business Media in 2005. At the time David joined as CEO, in the words of business journalist Patrick Smith, UBM was known as an "inky, fairly old-fashioned publisher with some strong print brands, some good events, a strange collection of legacy businesses left over from a previous era and no real direction." David's contribution was to transform that company into a competitive B2B organization. In the eight years under his leadership, UBM completed more than a hundred acquisitions and got rid of more than a dozen old businesses. The changing communications environment has had a major impact on the media business but UBM's success has been a testimony to its ability to adapt and transform itself.

In a way, the market disruption provided the impetus for UBM to redefine itself for the Social Age. But then, David had always been an advocate of change and the need to build organizations that can adapt to change through transformation. When we met him at his office, David quoted Bill Sharp, who helped him with scenario planning at Symbian and later at UBM: "When it rains in the Himalayas, it's going to flood in the plains three months later." The same lessons had to be applied to UBM, and David realized he had to transform UBM from a disparate group of companies into a cohesive community.

It Is the Community That Transforms

David's passion for community and purpose, and his endeavors to make sure that people do not feel disenfranchised, go back to 1965, when he came to the United Kingdom at the age of two with his family as a refugee "with no rights and knowing no one." Some of the biggest lessons that he was to channel through his own Personal Narrative as a leader came from his parents. His father, Archie Levin, was a political journalist who wrote against apartheid in South Africa. His writings invoked the wrath of the apartheid government and forced Mr. Levin and his family to flee. David has never forgotten how an alien society opened its doors and absorbed his family into its fold, and it continues to be a driving force in his efforts to create company cultures where people feel a sense of belonging and purpose. David's mother, Leah Levin, went on to become a luminary in the world of human rights and development and was given an OBE (Order of the British Empire) for her work. David went on to marry a woman named Lindsay, who founded Leaders' Quest in 2001 to connect and inspire leaders from all walks of life in an effort to address pressing global issues. The notion of a global community is never far from David's life.

When David took over UBM in 2005, it was a motley collection of businesses. Business analysts have written extensively about the strategies he employed to turn the business into a highly profitable one. Less has been written about how David transformed the thinking and leadership, that guided the UBM staff. He had to focus on culture, and he started making deep changes thereby creating what he refers to as "new neural wiring."

David's first lessons on leadership were at the age of twenty-eight when he was the managing director of a small manufacturing firm with a deeply fractured culture. "That's where I learned about culture and its importance. Imagine a place where there were three varieties of toilet papers for three grades of staff," he says. It was in this culture that David learned the value of building a community and that "there is such a thing as leadership." "It is in who you are," David says with passion, "it is about your authenticity."

That single-minded drive to authenticity has stayed with David all the way through, and he brought that into his role as CEO of UBM. "Culture is everything," is one of David's favorite phrases, and he tends to his company's culture with the care of an expert gardener tending the soil: "... unless there is a neural network in an organization that is fast, quick, and intelligent, the organization does not transform and cannot keep pace with the changes outside. Those in the neural network have got to have belief, hope, empowerment, and they become the missionaries for the organization."

Jenny Duvalier, now head of people and culture at the technology innovation giant ARM holdings, was at that time UBM's head of people and culture and, was instrumental in converting David's gut feelings and raw ideas into action. Jenny brought her own passion for dialogue, respect, clarity, and agility into the mix, and her partnership with David led them to create the neural network through a business leadership program (BLP) for all senior leaders at UBM. This was the crucial first step toward driving change by building a community. One of the authors remembers the time in 2012 when David turned up to speak to a group of UBM senior managers who were on their BLP journey, managed by Duke Corporate Education. On a wintry morning in San Francisco, David sat in a circle and told his story. Plainly and candidly, he spoke of himself and what drove him. He talked of his family, his sons, the mistakes he had made in his life, his struggles, and his vision for the company and for the world. For an hour, the group was transfixed, listening to a CEO who spoke about his values and his own journey in life. That evening, a participant commented on how she had felt as though she was suddenly part of a community with a common story. She had learned the power of purpose.

The Hub as Community

David was very clear from the time he took over that UBM's business was about the communities it served, and therefore community building had to become its heart and soul. He had three simple guide-lines for the culture he wanted to create at UBM:

1. Develop a culture that helps people collaborate
2. Become a learning organization addicted to change
3. Connect people to compound expertise and opportunity

Jenny Duvalier commented that, for David, "the community-centric approach was personal as well as driven by a strategic rationale: he believes strongly in the power of community to provide learning, sup-port, and enrichment." Jenny described to us the culture that was there when David joined as CEO: silo-focused, tribal, un-collaborative, and adversarial (in some places). "Over the years, and with David's very personal role modeling, we tried to show that there was a different way to interact, that was good for both our customers and our colleagues," she says. Jenny refers to David as having played two roles at UBM: not only was he the CEO, he was also the chief community officer!

The Hub, UBM's online community platform, is helping UBM achieve exactly that. According to UBM community manager Ted Hopton, these are the three defining points of a community: one, the insiders feel a sense of connection with one another; two, they feel a sense of empowerment; and three, like good neighbors they care for and support one another.

The Hub's roots go back to the year 2008, when a wiki was used for an executive off-site meeting. Participants at the meeting found it helped them to collaborate, but the organization continued to be deeply divided. As Ted says, "The very fact that different parts of UBM were called divisions was testimony to how divided it was!" The watershed moment took place when David wrote his first blog post, and soon the blog replaced his monthly e-mails. A conversation began between the CEO and the employees of UBM. People were suddenly empowered to participate in the community.

By 2009, a major division of UBM had replaced mass e-mails with the platform's blog. In 2010, when the Icelandic volcano ash crisis dis-rupted travel for several days, the Hub became a critical crisis commu-nication tool. In the same year, the company executive summit started using the Hub, and later in the year UBM made a major acquisition and the Hub became the key platform for onboarding new members of the UBM community. By the end of the year, the blog posts and comments had increased by 40 percent. In 2012, UBM Asia committed to using the Hub for all of its official communication, and when Hurricane Sandy shut down e-mail, servers, phones, and offices in the United States, the Hub kept employees connected and working. Today, more than 70 percent of employees are active on the Hub! It is truly a community.

THE ARCHITECTURE OF A COMMUNITY

Drawing on the lessons of UBM and many other companies we have worked with over the years, we have found that there is a common architectural style to businesses that operate as communities. Here are the principles we find:

FIGURE 2-3 Community Principles

Membership

Membership principles are concerned with how individuals join with and feel a part of the community.

Self-Selection: Increasingly, community members will look for greater say in projects and assignments, creating a need to balance the passions of the individual with the needs of the organization.

Fluid roles: Members of the community need to be able to move through different roles as needs arise, to create the agility to respond to unforeseen events.

Fluid membership: Individuals will move in and out of the community more frequently than ever before: return trips will become common rather than notable, and need to be encouraged.

Opinion leadership: An individual member can have great influence within a community even without a formal position of authority. The ability to harness social energy and move the members of the community to action will increasingly be vested in those whose ideas are galvanizing and whose approaches are productive from a Social Leadership perspective.

Affinity

Affinity principles are concerned with the enablement of community members.

Ownership: Core processes and projects continue to have accountable individuals or teams—often with special expertise—however, community members expect to have input into and share "ownership" of these processes. It becomes *our* budget process rather than *the* budget process or *finance's* budget requirements.

Voice: Community members are actively engaged in setting the rules by which the organization operates. Some of these may become formalized; others exist as community standards or norms. Further, community members tend to find others with similar interests and ideas. Although there are common interests across the community, each affinity grouping may develop its own point of view, communicate this across the organization, and attempt to influence the company's overall agenda.

Personal development: Members of the community expect that the community will help them grow and develop in ways of their choosing, consistent with the goals of the community. Communities create opportunities for their members to develop and improve themselves both formally and informally.

Connectivity

Connectivity principles are concerned with the relation of community members to outside communities.

Porous borders: The borders of a community are at the same time very clear and very porous. Communities have ways of letting people from outside lend their expertise and resources while at the same time being clear about who is and who is not a member.

Talent fluency: Members know one another. Within a community, members come to know who can be relied on, as well as who has what skills and what level of commitment to different activities. There is a certain "talent fluency"—widespread knowledge about who is capable of what. It is very difficult, almost impossible, to be an anonymous member of a community. Communities by their nature seek active engagement.

External accountability: Communities recognize their responsibility to other communities. Communities that thrive and survive do so in part because they recognize their interconnection to the other communities within their sphere.

These three areas—membership, affinity, and connectivity—are the building blocks that allow people within a community to create the systems and conditions that bring them together as a group to accomplish their objectives.

Let's take a brief look at how these principles contrast with those found in traditional, bureaucratic organizations.

	Bureaucratic Organization	Business Community Principle	Business Community Adaptation
Core Capability	Control of resources, means of production, and decision making	Expansion and acceleration of Social Energy	Participation by members in the generation of Social Energy
Members	Selection into the organization and into different departments actively driven by "management," passively participated in by the individual, and occurs episodically Everyone has a job Decision to leave a department or organization considered a milestone; returns rare Leaders are those in formal roles, members make suggestions or "contributions"	Self-selection Fluid roles Fluid membership Opinion leadership	Selection into the organization and its different parts actively driven by both the leaders and the members, and is ongoing Everyone moves through different roles as needs arise Decisions to leave the department or the organization considered natural; returns expected Anyone with a valid idea can influence the course of events
Affinity	Employees accountable for delivering objectives agreed on with boss Top management determines polices	Ownership Voice Personal development	Members accountable for doing whatever needs to be done to enable the business to grow Members influence and contribute to policy and strategy

(Continued)

33

	Bureaucratic Organization	Business Community Principle	Business Community Adaptation
	"Management" decides who works with whom The organization opens up development opportunities and the individual is accountable for taking advantage of them		The organization opens up development opportunities and the individual is accountable for taking advantage of them
Connectivity	Employees of the company or department are clear about who is "us" and who is "them"—others are kept at arm's length Managers and employees know their own group well, with little knowledge of those in other groups Organizations and departments know and operate within the rules, so that all companies compete fairly	Porous borders Talent fluency External accountability	Members are clear about other members and work in partnership with anyone who can help Knowing talent, beyond one's daily interactions, is considered part of "good citizenship" Communities understand their accountability to the environments in which they operate and their need to be actively engaged with other organizations

Moving toward a community model from that of a traditional organization involves two things. At one level, it involves extending and accelerating some trends that are already occurring today, such as the socialization of information, thinking of networks as the fundamental unit to be addressed, and dealing with prosumers who want to be seen as constituents of the organization and have a voice in the company's activities. At a second level, it means rethinking leadership—moving toward a model of the leader as mayor.

SUMMARY

The forces of the Social Age not only affect the way we lead and the way individuals relate in the world but, in fact, are changing the very nature of the companies in which we work. Once, hierarchical structures based on the metaphor of the military formed the ideal balance of structure and centralization. Today, flattened structures of networked groups align within the metaphor of a community to best address the needs of the Social Age. Making this transformation involves adopting a set of principles, which we call Community Principles. These include:

Membership

Self-Selection
Fluid roles
Fluid membership
Opinion leadership

Affinity

Ownership
Voice
Personal development

Connectivity

Porous borders
Talent fluency
External accountability

These three areas—membership, affinity, and connectivity—are the building blocks that allow people within a community to create the systems and conditions that bring them together as a group to accomplish their objectives.

3

The Leader as Mayor

Leadership should be born out of the understanding of the needs of those who would be affected by it.

MARIAN ANDERSON

In the previous chapter we talked about business as a community rather than as a bureaucracy, and we looked at UBM as an example of a company that successfully made the switch to a community. Our premise for advancing the community model is that the traditional bureaucratic model is fast becoming obsolete in the Social Age. This is an age in which information is ubiquitous, and it's one in which there are no barriers to influencing both the creation and meaning of information, constantly and in real time.

SOCIAL ENERGY

Earlier we introduced the term "Social Energy," a key resource in the Social Age. If intellectual capital was the resource that marked the Information Age, it is Social Energy that marks the Social Age. We came up with this term after interviewing more than five hundred people in twenty-four organizations that cut across diverse sectors and industries. We asked these people to describe the chief resources they felt were critical to succeeding in the Social Age. The characteristics that recurred most often were: passion, curiosity, engagement, connectedness, decisiveness, awareness, meaning, drive, empathy, agility, and purpose. When we looked at our results, we felt we were staring at something very important. There was a significant tilt toward words that were loaded with emotive content and social connectivity. Not that intellectual capital, know-how, knowledge, and so on were considered irrelevant; rather, it was taken for granted that these resources existed. It was as if the participants were looking at the next stage of evolution and saying that knowledge without a social and emotive component was becoming irrelevant.

One participant from Barclays Bank at a "top fifty leaders" workshop, described the resources needed as a "...kind of energy that needs to be in my company, something that holds us together in the absence of all the old hooks, and invites the customer to become part of it." It was precisely this energy that Andrea Jung, the erstwhile CEO of Avon during its heyday, was able to generate, and every employee felt its presence.

But Social Energy is not new; leaders have created it and tapped into it for several generations. All we are saying is that it is becoming more critical than ever. One of the most celebrated examples of tapping into Social Energy is that of Nelson Mandela bringing together a deeply divided nation after the African National Congress came to power. He had the easier option to retaliate against the previous apartheid government and to seize back assets from the minority that had ruled South Africa for so long. He chose the more difficult path of reconciliation, allowing the perpetrator to seek forgiveness and be forgiven by the victim in a reconciliation court. Doing this created the possibility for black and white South Africans to generate a sense of emotional engagement within the larger context of building a nation.

Another example is the way Mandela chose powerful symbolic action to generate Social Energy at a Rugby World Cup final. The Springboks rugby team was long considered a symbol of racism and apartheid by the black majority of the newly formed republic. Once the African National Congress came to power, there were clarion calls to ban the team. Not only was Mandela against banning the team, he wore the Springbok colors to the World Cup final, striding out to the middle of the ground to meet the players. Black and white South Africans cheered together for the Springboks as they stormed to victory, and a simple symbolic action became the harbinger of a Social Energy that swept across the new country, touching each and every citizen.

In chapter 8 we will discuss the challenge of relating authentically to deeply connected constituencies and will explore the conversations, actions, and behaviors a leader needs to exhibit to generate an upward, positive cycle of Social Energy. For now, as we introduce the full score of Social Leadership, let's begin by examining the underlying principles of shifting your leadership approach to be more like a mayor's and less like a general's.

THE SOCIAL LEADER'S FIELD OF ACTION

What Nelson Mandela was doing in bringing South Africa together was balancing two powerful sets of forces that impact all of us: one, the need for certainty versus the need to tolerate ambiguity; and two, focusing on people versus focusing on tasks. Take a small rubber band. Imagine that the space within this rubber band represents all of the room in which you have to maneuver as a leader. Now take your thumb and index finger and stretch the rubber band. It has gotten longer but narrower. You may have improved your room to maneuver in some ways but limited it in others. Now take your other thumb and index finger, insert them crosswise into the stretched rubber band, and spread them as well. You now have a broad square, a much larger field of action. Perhaps it looks something like this:

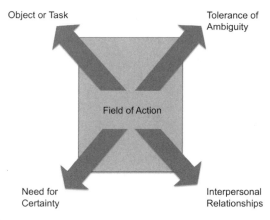

FIGURE 3-1 Field of Action

Balancing the dynamic tensions within these four poles—ambiguity, certainty, people, and tasks—creates a broad field of action. John D. Ingalls was among the first to describe this set of forces. He described them as follows:[1]

Need for certainty:
- The search for cognitive balance or consistency (logic)
- The tendency for social evaluation and comparison (judgment)
- Attribution and the assignment of motives (assumption)

Tolerance of ambiguity:
- The capacity for remaining open to experience (acceptance)
- The ability to be descriptive (nonjudgmental assessment)
- The willingness to question and inquire (experiment and exploration)

Focus on tasks:
- Positioning one's role through the objective lens of task

Focus on people:
- Positioning one's role through the subjective lens of relationship

Our goal as Social Leaders is to focus on all four poles, so that we live within this dynamic tension to create the most space to lead and bring constituencies together.

Ingalls describes how, for too long, leaders have focused on only half of this field of action, concerned with driving tasks and building certainty; we would call this operating as generals. As we have discussed, in today's reality this is a fool's errand. As a leader you must balance all of these forces and, like a mayor, pay attention to people as well as tasks and accept ambiguity while searching for some solid ground of certainty. The psychologist Carl Jung called the capacity to create this balance the *transcendent function of consciousness.*[2] We call it being a Social Leader. Jung encouraged people to seek this balance by understanding how they perceive the world. We add that it is crucial to also understand how you act upon the world to influence those around you.

THE LEADER AS MAYOR

If, in a traditional organization, the successful leader was a general, focusing on certainty and task, then in the community-based organizations of the Social Age the successful leader will be a mayor, focusing on all four poles of the field of action—certainty, ambiguity, tasks, and people. The differences between generals and mayors are immediately obvious:

- Generals have troops; mayors have constituents
- Generals are known by their troops; mayors know their constituents
- Generals command; mayors influence

Generals lead by command based on their position in the hierarchy, which they achieved independent of the wishes of their troops; mayors govern from their position in the community, which they achieve with the consent of their constituents.

Constituents versus troops, knowing versus being known, governing versus commanding, consent-based influence versus positional

Traditional Organization

"Community-Based" Organization

- The leader was:
  - A General directing the troops
  - Setting strategy building organizational alignment
  - Directing execution and continuous improvement

- The leader is:
  - A *Mayor* addressing the needs of constituencies
  - Inspiring common purpose
  - Harnessing *Social Energy*

FIGURE 3-2 Generals vs. Mayors

authority: these are the new realities of leading within a community-based business. But how do leaders succeed within these new realities? The traditional answer to this question has been to focus on establishing correct patterns of behavior—competency models, if you will—that instruct the leader how to act and provide the organization with standards for assessing leadership. We find this approach to be challenged in several areas because it relies on leaders adopting ways of behaving that may not resonate with who they are authentically and that artificially constrict what a leader can do to be effective.

We believe that the answer is not a set pattern of behavior or a rigid "competency model." Creating a fixed list of successful leadership behaviors runs the risk of being quickly out of date, ineffectively simplistic or bewilderingly lengthy.

The United Nations, for instance, has a complete set of forty-three "core competencies" plus another forty managerial competencies that provide a rich and bewildering smorgasbord of all the wonderful behaviors the organization wants to track, monitor, and measure in its people and managers. An entire machinery remains in operation at the UN to sustain the production, upkeep, and implementation of this competency framework. The outcome of this mammoth endeavor to

From: Fit the Mold

- Focus on "what the leader does"
  - Identify the "right" behaviors
  - Teach leaders these behaviors
  - Reinforce these behaviors through rewards and feedback

Toward: Be Authentic

- Focus on "what the leader is capable of"
  - Understand "who" the leader is
  - Grow the productive aspects of the leader
  - Reinforce continuous adaptive changes in behavior through rewards and feedback

FIGURE 3-3   Fitting the Mold vs. Being Authentic

reduce human development into a neat set of measurable parameters remains dubious.

It is a fine idea to have a list of values that all employees should aspire toward. However, our experience tells us that while competency models look great on paper, a far more effective approach is to encourage leaders to become the most productive version of the person they are meant to be. Or to use the famous words of psychologist Abraham Maslow, "A musician must make music, an artist must paint, a poet must write; if he is to be ultimately at peace with himself, what a man can be, he must be."

TENETS OF SOCIAL LEADERSHIP

We do, however, need a framework as the basis for a common understanding of how each of us can develop as a Social Leader. The framework must include all four poles suggested by Ingalls in his field of action. We propose that as an alternative to competency models we instead look at a framework that describes "who the leader is." This allows each one of us the flexibility of using behaviors (and conversations and actions) that are uniquely productive for us while allowing a common basis for describing the areas of focus for success. We call this framework the Tenets of Social Leadership and suggest that there are five core Tenets. Success as a leader is based on understanding these five core tenets with regard to oneself, and learning to capitalize on one's own most productive aspects within these five tenets.

The five tenets for becoming a successful Social Leader that we want to focus on are:

Mindfulness: maintaining and acting on four types of awareness: Temporal awareness, Situational awareness, Peripheral awareness, and Self-awareness.

Proactivity: the belief that one is in control of one's own actions and seeing oneself as being able to influence events rather than being dragged along by them

43

Authenticity: engendering in others a belief in your own credibility; the ability to build personal trust in a relationship and positively confront disagreement and competing points of view

Openness to learning, growth, and ambiguity: the capacities to act, thrive, and learn from situations that are complex, novel, and ambiguous

Social scalability: fluidly communicating separately and jointly to: one individual, a small group, the entire organization

These five Tenets of Social Leadership interact in a dynamic way to form an individual leader's *Personal Narrative.* A Personal Narrative is the thematic story describing an individual that 1) the individual believes about himself and 2) that others believe about that person. Others experience our Personal Narrative through our conversations, actions, and behaviors (CABs). In the following chapters we will explore the concept of conversations, actions, and behaviors as leadership in action based on the underlying Tenets of Social Leadership.

Social Leadership: Influencing & Leading Constituencies

FIGURE 3-4 Social Leader Tenets

44

For now, let's explore the basis of Social Leadership and what this means for your own Personal Narrative.

OUR INTERNAL THEATER

We use the idea of an "internal theater" to denote aspects of you as leader that are within yourself. Mindfulness and proactivity help the leader remain purposeful and aware of the conversations, actions, and behaviors she uses in leading others. Both these tenets share the characteristic that they are fully within the leader—they are part of one's own internal theater. In large part, though not exclusively, they help determine that part of the leader's Personal Narrative that he tells about himself.

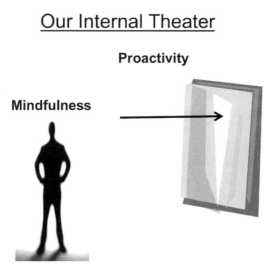

Our Internal Theater

Proactivity

Mindfulness

The characteristic way in which we seek to approach the world – independent of the immediate situation; our internal dialogue

FIGURE 3-5   Internal Theater

Mindfulness

Mindfulness allows a leader to purposely set his course of action, recognize his actions' impact on others, and adjust them accordingly. We think of mindfulness as having four aspects:

- **Self-awareness**—knowing your strengths and weaknesses and being able to see the impact of your behavior on others
- **Situational awareness**—reading the situation accurately and synchronizing one's conversations, actions, and behaviors to the needs of the moment
- **Peripheral awareness**—being able to "keep an eye" on the horizon and detect weak signals, early warning signs of trends that will have an impact over time even if they do not at the moment
- **Temporal awareness**—staying in the moment and recognizing when your reactions are driven from past events rather than present events

Proactivity

Proactivity concerns a leader's ability to see herself as the initiator of events rather than the responder. To some extent this tenet has to do with the way a leader sees herself as capable and potent to influence a situation or challenge. To a greater extent, though, it is about the way a leader perceives situations and challenges—does she see them as a field on which to exert her capabilities or as an interconnected set of events to which she is a spectator. As Fred Kofman, author of *Conscious Business* puts it, does the leader see himself as a player or a victim?[3]

OUR EXTERNAL THEATER

We use the idea of "external theater" to denote those aspects of your leadership that involve engaging with others. Authenticity and openness focus on the ways that we initiate and respond to the people we choose to influence and lead.

Authenticity and Openness

Authenticity and openness are aspects of the leader that involve engagement with others. These two tenets in large part, though again not exclusively, determine the part of the leader's Personal Narrative to which others have access.

Authenticity refers to the quality of relationship that the leader is able to engender with her constituents. It is built on a leader's capacity to create an atmosphere of trust through consistent, unbiased action and to display empathy without being seen as basing decisions on sympathy. Let's look at an example of building trust and credibility by comparing two leaders, C-suite executives with whom one of the authors has worked: Leader A has been able to demonstrate the productive aspects of authenticity and Leader B has not. When something important goes wrong and needs to be brought to the leader's attention, the constituents of Leader A respond by saying, "Let's go tell

Our External Theater

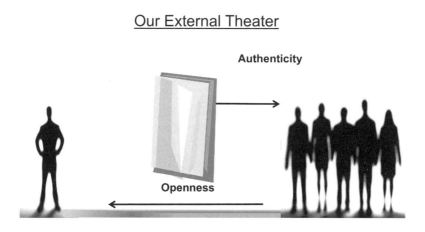

Authenticity

Openness

The characteristic ways we act in the world – our response to the situations and people we encounter; our conversations, behaviors and actions

FIGURE 3-6   External Theater

47

Leader A." Conversely, the constituents of Leader B respond by asking, "How should we tell Leader B?" Leader A consistently learned of problems quickly and fully, while Leader B learned of problems more slowly and with "spin" that forced him to work much harder to gain a full and accurate appreciation for what was going on. Over time this had a significant impact on the success of Leader B.

Openness to Learning, Growth, and Ambiguity

Just as leaders' actions affect those around them, they are in turn subject to the actions of their constituents. The tenet of openness to learning, growth, and ambiguity refers to the aspect of the leader that allows him to experience information, experiences, and situations as new, with a positive, embracing attitude.

Psychologists have pointed out that we all look at the world seeking familiar patterns to help us quickly sort through the vast amount of information that bombards us. Once we recognize an event as essentially similar to a past experience, we know how to deal with it with a minimum of thought.[4] We each have our own awareness point— that point where we see something as different enough from our past experience to recognize it as new. The positive aspects of openness are those that allow us to have an appropriately set awareness point— one that is low enough to make us appreciate the novelty around us without becoming overwhelmed. Of course, seeing something as new is only one half of the equation. The other half is embracing the novel experience and seeking to use it as an opportunity to learn and grow.

OUR STAGE

Our internal and external theater performances play out on a stage. Our stage operates like our own personal YouTube channel where the world can tune in as it chooses. As leaders we must be prepared to speak to any range of audience at any moment, and to speak while they are speaking to each other. We call this capability *Social Scalability*.

Our Stage

Social Scalability

Our ability to easily shift the scale on which we lead; our ability
to successfully influence and communicate when working with
individuals, teams and entire organizations.

FIGURE 3-7 Stage

Social Scalability

The final tenet of Social Leadership, social scalability, refers to the
stage on which the leader is working and his ability to transition easily from one stage to the next. In the Social Age, "who" the leader is
dealing with is not always within her control. At the same time, the
expectation that the leader will be available to a widespread constitu-
ency is higher than ever. In this context, a leader will need to display
the other tenets—mindfulness, authenticity, personal agency, and
openness—and make smooth and easy transitions among audiences,
from one person to a team and the entire community.

Think of those leaders you've met who have this ability to influence people across the organizational spectrum, from those on the
shop floor to those in the boardroom. What exactly do they do differently? Their message and the core story remain the same, what varies
is their ability to connect with different people differently. Leaders
who do that are able to fine-tune their message to reach different

audiences. This demands a high level of empathy on their part. They work to recognize that the underlying experiences that shaped the way they see the world may be different from the experiences of those hearing their message.

Mayor–leaders also recognize that in the Social Age everyone they speak with has a megaphone. Their audience is able to—and even expects to—share not only the leader's message but their own view point on it. And these multiple viewpoints spread virally. Transparency and communal conversation are the new normal.

YOUR PERSONAL NARRATIVE

These five leadership tenets are the building blocks of an individual's Personal Narrative. Successful leaders have Personal Narratives that are aligned and that have productive themes. By aligned we mean that the way the individual sees himself is the way others see him. The stories that the leader tells about her leadership experiences are thematically similar to those that are told by her constituents.

By productive we refer to the character of the conversations, actions, and behaviors (CABs) the leader displays within each of the five tenets. Each of the tenets can have productive and unproductive aspects, and a leader will at times display productive or unproductive aspects of each tenet. The goal of a successful leader is to understand which aspects of each tenet are most consistently characteristic of him and then to work on capitalizing on the productive aspects and developing strategies for compensating for the unproductive aspects.

In part 2 we will dive deeply into each tenet and explore how you can use it to productively address the challenges of the Social Age as well as learn to recognize and expand your own productive capabilities in each. For now, if you want to quickly gain a deeper feel for each of the tenets, have a look at the appendix, which provides a sample list of characteristically productive and unproductive CABs for each of the five Tenets of Social Leadership.

IN SUMMARY

So far we have demonstrated seven crucial points.

1. We are living in a Social Age, a time defined by digital technology, globalization, and an expectation of participation by everyone who cares about a topic. Most of us are immigrants to this world, and bring with us a mind-set of leadership and organizations developed before the dawn of global digital social connectivity.

2. In this Social Age we see: the socialization of information, with points of view created continually, communally, and in real time; the rise of global, networked communities linked through technology and now operating as a fundamental unit of analysis to be addressed; and the rise of the prosumer, individuals and communities both inside and outside of companies that expect to have a voice in the company's strategy and actions.

3. The Social Age is creating a number of leadership challenges, some of which are new and all of which are new in their intensity:
   ○ Anticipating discontinuity
   ○ Remaining proactive in the face of ambiguity
   ○ The demands of connected constituents
   ○ Dealing with social information
   ○ Communicating when everyone has a megaphone

4. These features and challenges of the Social Age are pushing organizations to operate more like communities and less like traditional hierarchies. This is causing a rethinking of some of the fundamental principles upon which companies operate, including how they think of members (employees), affinity (participation and engagement), and connectivity (relationships beyond the company).

5. Importantly, the shift to community-based organizational structures embedded in the Social Age means a shift in thinking about leadership. Leaders can no longer be generals commanding troops and

setting strategy; instead, they must be mayors, influencing constituencies and reacting to unforeseen events.

6. In this new reality of the mayor–leader it is important to focus on the productive capabilities of the individual leader, her Personal Narrative, rather than on a fixed set of behaviors.

7. A leader's Personal Narrative is best understood through the lens of the Tenets of Social Leadership:
- Mindfulness
- Proactivity
- Authenticity
- Openness
- Social scalability

Now let's look at you in terms of the Tenets of Social Leadership and see what you can do to expand your own productive conversations, actions, and behaviors in each of these areas.

4

Understanding Yourself
as a Social Leader

O wad some Power the giftie gie us
To see oursels as ithers see us!

ROBERT BURNS

So far we've looked at the five core challenges of the Social Age and at the Tenets of Social Leadership necessary to address these challenges. These next two chapters focus on you, describing how you can begin to increase the productive conversations, actions, and behaviors that we described in the Tenets of Social Leadership.

We begin by looking at how you can understand "who you are" in terms of Social Leadership, helping you understand when you are most productive as a leader in dealing with the new realities of the Social Age. Next, we will look at how you can grow the productive aspects of your leadership in a way that maintains your authenticity, that is, growing those aspects of your leadership that are already productive. Finally, we will look at what you can do as a mayor-leader to foster an environment that generates and capitalizes on Social Energy, helping your organization to operate more like a community.

Let's begin by better understanding yourself as a Social Leader. We are going to do three things:

1. Help you understand how to look at your Personal Narrative
2. Provide you with tools to uncover your Personal Narrative
3. Give you the tools to use your Personal Narrative to assess yourself as a Social Leader

The tools and process will look like this:

FIGURE 4-1   Discovery Process

It's important to emphasize that these tools and this process simply offer a way to organize information and think about yourself. The Tenets of Social Leadership are a lens through which to view your own productive leadership capabilities.

We asked Jonathan Donner, VP of Global Learning and Capability Development at Unilever, what he has learned over the years about his own style of leadership. Here is what he said: "If I had to summarize, it would be a realization that over time leadership and careers should be based on mindful decisions, choices, ownership; it is highly personal and individual. I think like many executives I'm becoming wise about the transition to self-definition and 'maturity.'"

We could not have said it better. As we noted at the outset, we view leadership much the way Jonathan does: "it is highly personal and individual." Being a successful leader in this Social Age requires capitalizing on the most productive aspects of who you are and maintaining a sense of authenticity. The tools and processes that follow in this chapter are guides to help you on your journey of self-discovery.

WHAT IS A PERSONAL NARRATIVE?

Your Personal Narrative is the intersection of the stories you tell about yourself and the stories others tell about you. All stories have two critical elements: themes and an arc.

Themes

Themes are recurring patterns; they appear when you look at a collection of your personal stories. We will use the lens of Social Leadership to look for and interpret the themes in your stories. But which stories about yourself should you look at? In their groundbreaking work on talent development, Morgan McCall and Michael Lombardo describe the critical nature of experience in our development.[1] The types of experiences they describe as developmental have one common feature: novelty. When we experience novelty, we find ourselves doing two things when the issues, people, or challenges we are confronted with do not fit into recognizable patterns.

First, novel situations force us to pay close attention and actively seek to understand what is in front of us rather than act automatically. This is because novel situations do not fit neatly into our expectations and established ways of responding. Second, we problem solve—we use our experience, existing capabilities, and the help of those around us to develop new ways of addressing the new challenges. Novel situations take us from a "static state" to one where everything is "in motion."

FIGURE 4-2 Personal Narrative

All too often, when we are in a static state we are only minimally aware of our characteristic beliefs, perceptions, and ways of behaving. When we are *in motion*, our beliefs, perceptions, and normal patterns of behavior get disrupted. These are important moments in your career, times when you became acutely aware of who you are, what you believe, and how you behave. We call these *seminal situations*. The stories you tell and the ones others tell about you during these seminal situations are perfect for understanding the Social Leader themes in your Personal Narrative.

The Learning Arc

All interesting narratives have a story arc, a rhythm and flow that carry us forward and help us understand how the characters evolve. To understand your arc as a Social Leader we are going to borrow a story arc from Joseph Campbell's book *The Hero with a Thousand Faces*, called the hero's journey.

But before we get there, let's follow the story of Luca.

LUCA'S JOURNEY

Luca had joined a leading food and beverage company as a young man and had impressed one and all with his desire to learn and his passion for sales. He rose steadily in his career, and by the age of thirty-five he was heading up sales for a large country in Eastern Europe. As luck would have it, Luca was fast-tracked into the role of general manager in an emerging market sooner than anyone would have deemed possible.

Luca found himself relocating with his young wife and child, excited about the future. The VP of the region gave him some advice on what to expect. He told Luca that he would have to learn quickly to deal with new players and groups over whom he didn't have direct authority. But he also assured Luca that his extroverted personality and ease with people would help him get along with everyone.

Luca loved the responsibility of the role and the challenges of succeeding in a new market, but he soon began complaining of the "endless meetings" and the matrix structure, which he felt was a waste of time. As the global economy went into a tailspin, a few countries in the market Luca headed were hit hard. The meetings grew longer and more frustrating, as none of the key contributors needed to drive change reported to Luca. He found two of them particularly difficult. One was the supply chain director, who was the same age as Luca and equally ambitious. What particularly irked Luca was that, instead of focusing on supplying products that the local market needed, the supply chain director would talk of global pipelines and the need to rationalize the global supply chain.

The other person Luca had difficulty with was the marketing director, who had a passion for using data and research; she got on Luca's nerves when she started questioning parts of the regional sales strategy, relying on data and advice from a leading consulting firm that was pointing them in a different direction. Both directors were based in the same office as Luca, but neither reported to him. Luca's struggles had just started.

As the pressure of being in a new role with very little authority began to rise, Luca's reaction was to go back to the behaviors that had made him successful previously. He started staying late in the office and expected others to rally around him. Those who couldn't work at Luca's pace soon became marginalized, and splinter groups began forming in the office. Luca repeatedly ignored e-mails from the supply chain and marketing directors and began having meetings without including them.

Luca's young wife felt adrift in a new country with few friends, and his long absences from home made things worse. One night, their young son came down with a high fever and had to be taken to the ICU in the local hospital for suspected meningitis. Luca rushed to the hospital from the office and spent the night outside the ICU with his wife. Tired and frustrated, he felt that so much in life was going against him. He felt angry and victimized, and believed no one at the office understood him. All he wanted was to make his company number one in the region, but the others didn't understand him at all.

At around 3 a.m., he got up from the plastic chair outside the ICU and went looking for the coffee machine. As he passed by a window in the half-lit corridor, a memory came back of an evening he had spent with his friend Sudheer. He remembered the words Sudheer had said to him after a lengthy conversation about life's struggles. "You are such a great guy in every way, Luca," Sudheer had said, "but you need to watch out for your ego. It's like you go into a shell when you don't want to listen and you just dig a hole there." Stung by the remark, Luca had lost touch with Sudheer. That was three years ago.

On impulse, Luca reached for his iPhone and sent Sudheer an e-mail asking how he was and mentioning that he was sending it from a hospital. Within a few minutes Sudheer had written back saying how much he'd thought of Luca in the past three years and how much he had missed their friendship. Something big seemed to shift inside Luca as he sipped his coffee, and he resolved to do something about his situation.

Two days later, Luca sought an appointment with the VP of the region. He talked of his failures and frustrations, making no attempt to hide his feelings. Luca asked the VP if he thought that Luca should offer to quit. The VP smiled and said, "When I met you ten years ago, I saw something in you that I still see. Let's work on these few issues." They spent the next four hours in conversation.

The following week, Luca invited the directors of supply chain and marketing for a meeting. The regional VP was present too. In the meeting, Luca was honest and authentic for the first time, and he explained how, in his passion for driving sales excellence, he had been myopic. He asked the two for feedback and listened intently when they told him that they felt marginalized and at sea. The group then talked of the pressures they were all under and agreed on a few ways they would try to make change happen. That evening they went for dinner, and for the first time Luca felt that he was part of a team.

Luca's story is an excellent example of what Joseph Campbell describes as "the hero's journey."[2] In Campbell's view, the hero's journey is the structure that underlies almost all mythology, from the stories of Osiris and Prometheus to those about Anakin and Luke Skywalker. In the hero's journey, a hero is called to adventure, struggles with accepting this call, receives aid, meets with a series of trials, atones for his past, receives a great gift or power, and returns to his home, where he uses his new gift or power for the good of all.

Campbell's eloquent seventeen-stage model is a bit too detailed for our purposes.[3] Other authors have simplified Campbell's insight and we will make an attempt to do so as well, creating what we will call a Learning Arc. The Social Leader Learning Arc consists of six parts:

- **Seminal situation**: a significant or defining career event occurs
- **Struggle**: this seminal situation causes difficulties that have not been encountered before
- **Help**: someone or some event provides new skills, learning, or insight to help overcome the struggle
- **Trial**: the new skills, learning, or insight is put to the test
- **Success**: the leader overcomes a set of obstacles and deals with success within the context of the current challenge
- **New state**: the leader now has a new set of learning, skills, or insights to apply broadly

Luca's story follows the arc of the hero's journey: he is the protagonist who has to struggle with the novelty of the GM role. Initially, Luca refuses to acknowledge that this is a seminal situation that challenges him to expand his usual CABs. As a result, he keeps going back to what had worked for him before: his default approach of taking charge and leading his team from the front. But this is a new world with constituencies, dotted lines, and diverse agendas for which the old approach was not working. As he becomes increasingly frustrated, Luca becomes increasingly defensive. It takes a crisis to shake him out of his state.

When Luca comes to realize his normal approach is not working, he seeks guidance from a trusted source. He then does three critical things: he recognizes the CABs that are not working, those focused on single-minded drive; he expands the use of other CABs he has, those focused on dealing with ambiguity; and he seeks help from his VP to support his use of CABs that are not part of his repertoire, namely humility.

Luca's story closely follows the Learning Arc we outlined at the beginning of the chapter. The vast majority of the critical experiences in our lives follow this story arc. We are going to use this six-part Learning Arc to uncover the core themes of your Personal Narrative.

As you can see, the Learning Arc starts with our hero, you, at a "static state." Then a *seminal situation* occurs. Once you are faced with this situation, you struggle with new challenges that will not yield to your normal way of doing things. As you become aware that your normal approach is not working, you become open to help and new ideas. This "teachable moment" opens the door to someone, something, or some circumstance that helps you grow and acquire new ways of thinking about or solving this challenge.

Armed with these new powers, you go forward to resolve the problems (or trials) inherent to this seminal situation. Based on your success in dealing with this situation, you are now ready to apply these new capabilities to a wider range of situations. This Learning Arc might occur over the course of a day, a project, or many years. It shows how you move from a familiar "steady state" through challenges and learning to a new state of leadership ability. The figure on the following page outlines the Social Leader Learning Arc.

By looking across your Learning Arcs from a number of different seminal situations you can begin to see a pattern—the themes of your Personal Narrative. That pattern will help you understand those productive aspects of the five Tenets of Social Leadership that are most characteristic of you and most useful in your efforts to lead. It will also show you those nonproductive aspects of the five tenets that are characteristic of you and which are derailing your leadership efforts.

Creating Your Personal Narrative

Very often, when we work with individual leaders, we help them create their Personal Narratives by interviewing them about seminal situations in their careers as well as interviewing those who work most closely with them. By doing this we construct a set of themes that the leaders see in themselves as well as themes that others see in them.

The Social Leader Learning Arc

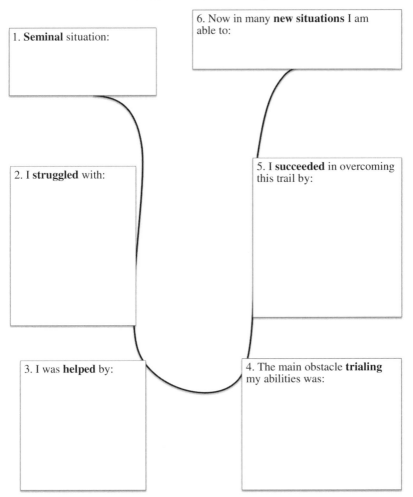

1. **Seminal** situation:

6. Now in many **new situations** I am able to:

2. I **struggled** with:

5. I **succeeded** in overcoming this trail by:

3. I was **helped** by:

4. The main obstacle **trialing** my abilities was:

FIGURE 4-3 Learning Arc

The overlap of themes—the Personal Narrative—is extremely useful in understanding the person as a Social Leader.

We would like to give you an opportunity to try this for yourself. Our own experience and much research by others over the years suggest that there are some common situations in the careers of leaders that tend to be seminal. We typically explore the following eight situations in an individual's work and life:

- Hardship
- Turnaround
- Start-ups
- New content/geography
- Changes in scope
- Leading without authority
- Overcoming resistance
- Major success

While most of these situations will be work related, it is frequently the case that some are personal or family related. Someone may relocate to follow a spouse or experience hardship through the loss of a loved one. All of these experiences shape who we are and how we lead.

At the end of this chapter we have provided a shorter version of the interview we often use. This interview contains, no surprise, eight items. Each item refers to one of the eight seminal situations above. For each situation there are a few follow-up questions to help you think fully about the situation. Try to put yourself back into your experience. Recall how it felt, what you thought, what you did that worked, and what didn't work. Importantly, try to recall what you did first: What were your first reactions and actions to the situation?

We have also provided a copy of the Social Leader Learning Arc at the end of this chapter. Make copies of this page. After you have thought about each situation fully, jot down some answers to each of the six questions on the Learning Arc. Each situation may take you as much as ten minutes to work through, and you may spend as much as ninety minutes on this effort. It will be worth it. When you are through, you will have completed notes on eight Learning Arcs. These are the stories you tell about yourself.

Of course, this is only one side of your Personal Narrative. Learning the stories others tell about the same situations is the important second half. It will be very difficult for you to interview a group of others about yourself. We suggest you do two things. First, take each of the eight Learning Arcs you have created and jot notes of things you have heard others say over the years about that situation. Be careful to note both comments that agree with what you have already written and those that are different. Try not to judge or discount the comments you have heard, just put them down.

Second, if you have one or two trusted colleagues or friends who you are comfortable with and believe would be honest with you, interview them. You can either interview them directly or give them the interview and ask that they write some notes and send it back to you. Once you have their answers, construct Learning Arcs from the notes. Make one Learning Arc for each situation, combining the notes from everyone you ask.

Uncovering Your Personal Narrative

Now that you have completed your eight Learning Arcs as well as additional Learning Arcs from trusted sources, read through each of them. Then review them as a group by reading all answers to each portion of the Learning Arc (that is, read the eight points on struggles, help, trials, and so on). Keep the questions below in mind as you read these arcs and identify recurring patterns, and use the Social Leadership Themes chart to take notes.

How do I see myself in the situation and in relation to other people, events, and time? When was I able to foresee critical events? When was I blindsided?

What drives me? How do I convey my values? How do I position my point of view with others? How have I reacted in ambiguous situations?

What is the quality and basis of my relationships? How do others respond to me? How do I respond when others challenge me?

How do I respond to new behavior from others? How do I learn?

In what circumstances am I most effective? In what social settings am I most comfortable?

SOCIAL LEADERSHIP PERSONAL THEMES

Use this chart to note common themes across all of your Learning Arcs.

Mindfulness: How do I try to see myself in the situation, in time and in relation to other people and events? When was I able to foresee critical events early? When was I blindsided?	
Productive	Nonproductive

Personal Agency: What drives me? How do I convey my value? How do I position my point of view with others? How have I reacted in ambiguous situations?	
Productive	Nonproductive

Authenticity: What is the quality & basis of my relationships? How do others respond to me? How do I respond when others challenge me?	
Productive	Nonproductive

Openness: How do I respond to new or novel behavior from others? How do I learn?	
Productive	Nonproductive

Social Scalability: In what circumstances am I most effective? In what social settings am I most comfortable?	
Productive	Nonproductive

Making Sense of Your Themes

First, it is important to recognize that no one is fully productive or fully unproductive in any of the five Tenets of Social Leadership. Most of us have aspects within each tenet in which we are productive, and we use these capabilities to address the challenges of the Social Age. Similarly, we each have areas that get in our way when dealing with these challenges. These unproductive CABs can cause us to stumble or fail.

In the appendix you will find a list of CABs that are indicative of being productive and unproductive as a Social Leader. Compare these CABs to the personal themes notes you took. Make a copy of the Social Leader Assessment Summary chart and, using the personal themes notes you created and the indicative CABs in the appendix, complete the summary. This summary will give you a clear picture of yourself as a Social Leader.

SOCIAL LEADER ASSESSMENT SUMMARY

	Mindfulness	Proactivity	Trust & Credibility	Openness	Social Scalability
Dealing with Disruption					
Remaining Proactive					
Communicating to Connected Constituencies					
Addressing real-time socially Created meaning					
Speaking when everyone has a megaphone					

Gut Check

Now what do you do with this understanding? Three things. First, ask yourself if this is truly you. Do the times, situations, and ways in which you have been productive and unproductive seem like you? Do the results you've experienced when leading others mesh with what you see here? Remember, you may not have thought about yourself in this way before, so it may feel like wearing a new pair of shoes. It may fit but not feel familiar.

Second, recognize areas where you are productive and consider situations where you could be applying these capabilities right now. Even though each of the tenets most directly addresses one of the key challenges of the Social Age, the others are still relevant. Are there productive areas that you could use right now to compensate for unproductive areas? Are there nonproductive CABs that you can begin to reduce?

Finally, it's time to think about growing those areas where you already have some productive capabilities. Are there areas where you have some productive capabilities that, with some focus and experience, could become towering strengths? The next chapter is all about creating a development plan to help you do just that.

IN SUMMARY

Having done the work in this chapter, you will have a strong sense of yourself as a Social Leader. You should have identified the productive and nonproductive aspects of the Tenets of Social Leadership that are characteristic of you and the way you lead others. The arcs, theme chart, and especially the Social Leader Assessment Summary you completed will provide a window into how you lead and interact with others, creating a detailed narrative of who you are as a Social Leader.

THE SOCIAL LEADER SELF-INTERVIEW

Instructions: Take some time and consider each of the eight situations and the questions that follow. Try to recall each incident with vivid detail. Then complete the Learning Arc for each situation. Take the time to write down the answers to the questions on the Learning Arc. Spend a full five to ten minutes on each situation (about sixty to ninety minutes in total for the full interview). You are worth it.

New Content/Geography
- Think about a time when you moved to a new country, city, or company. (If you have never moved, think about a time you moved into a new area of your business.) What were the first steps you took in that situation? Why?
  - How did you go about finding your feet?
  - What were the priorities you set up for yourself?
  - Do you find ways of coping with uncertain and ambiguous situations? How exactly did you go about it?

Change in Scope
- Think about a time when you had a major change in responsibility, for example, when you took over a division, assumed responsibility for a large staff, or took over a large client.
  - How did you set about establishing your presence?
  - What were your priorities?
  - What did your ninety-day plan look like?

Turnaround
- Think about an experience you've had when you had to quickly step in and clean up a mess, right a failing piece of the business, or manage a critical change.
  - How did you approach the problem?
  - What was uppermost in your mind?
  - How did you deal with the pressures that the turnaround/change brought?

Responsibility Without Authority
- Think of a situation where you were accountable for an important deliverable but did not have complete authority.
  - What strategies did you use to deal with this situation?
  - How did you work with those whose outputs were critical but over whom you had no authority?

Dealing with Resistance
- Think about a time when you were faced with resistance to your ideas or initiatives and the stakes were significant.
  - What and with whom did you communicate?
  - What frustrated you most about the situation?
  - Why do you think people were resisting you?
  - What were the first actions you took?

Promotion Within a Peer Group
- Consider a situation where you were promoted and had to lead a team of people that now include your former peers.
  - How did you manage the change in relationship?
  - What did you learn from that experience?
  - How would you do it differently if you were in that situation again?

Major Success
- Think about a critical success you achieved in your professional life.
  - What drove you to get to that point?
  - What were your main motivators?
  - What inspired you?

Failure/Hardship
- Consider a time when you encountered failure or went through a significant hardship.
  - What went wrong?
  - How did you find yourself coping with the hardships?
  - How did you manage to deal with the difficulties you encountered?
  - What did you learn about yourself from that situation?
  - Where did you find comfort?

The Social Leader Learning Arc

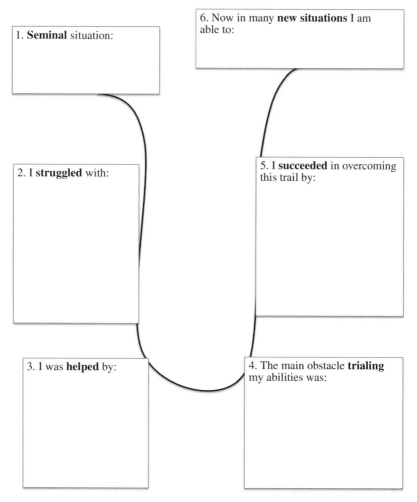

1. **Seminal** situation:

2. I **struggled** with:

3. I was **helped** by:

4. The main obstacle **trialing** my abilities was:

5. I **succeeded** in overcoming this trail by:

6. Now in many **new situations** I am able to:

5

Becoming More: Developing Yourself as a Social Leader

I am not what happened to me, I am what I choose to become.
CARL JUNG

Some years ago, one of the authors was working with the CEO and his team in a well-known pharmaceutical company. The problem was Colin. The senior vice president of research and development, Colin had previously been a member of the management team of a small but successful pharma R&D start-up before it was bought by this global organization four years earlier. Although he was happy when the deal went through, Colin was now struggling in his role in the large global corporation. He had acquired a reputation in the short time after the acquisition as being unapproachable, which is clearly at loggerheads with one of the competencies the company defines for his role—an "open and collaborative attitude."

The head of talent recommended that Colin work with an executive coach, which he did (although reluctantly). The results after a year were disappointing, though not for lack of effort. Colin tried to incorporate some behavioral changes that the coach recommended, such as trying to look approachable at meetings, keeping the door to his office open, and asking inquiring questions of others. After six months or so, he felt he was appearing stilted and awkward, as though he was doing what was not core to him. In short, he felt he was faking it.

Now, there is no doubt that some of these corrective behaviors might have helped Colin in the short run to improve others' perceptions of him. But these corrections weren't sustainable; maintaining behaviors that do not have an origin in who we actually are is difficult and over time can be seen as inauthentic. Behaving in a way that was foreign to him only made Colin seem even less approachable and further eroded others' views of him.

BECOMING THE SOCIAL LEADER

Colin's story will be familiar to any of us who have been given a list of new behaviors that would help us "improve." The organization wanted Colin to change his behavior and become more approachable. Colin tried, but could not hold it up in the long run. Something inside him was not in tune with the changes he was trying to make. Does that mean that Colin is doomed to remain "unapproachable"? No.

What Colin needs to do is become aware of the productive conversations, actions, and behaviors (CABs) that are already a part of him. He can start by looking at the root issue: What problems are his perceived lack of approachability causing? Colin can then extend the volume and scope of his productive CABs to address the difficulties his lack of approachability is causing. So, Colin is going to overcome a behavior pattern not by trying to mold himself to a fixed organizational competence, but by expanding and adapting his own repertoire of conversations, actions, and behaviors. Think of jujitsu as an alternative to boxing!

We are aware that we are sidestepping one of the dominant practices in the field of leadership development: the competency development model. Leadership competency models look great on paper. We believe, however, their fixed and retrospective nature makes them fraught with peril in the Social Age. Instead, we propose the following:

1. You can improve your capacity to lead successfully in the Social Age by increasing the volume and scope of the produc-

tive conversations, actions, and behaviors that are already part of you.

2. You can help yourself grow in this way by purposefully approaching challenging situations.
3. As growth tends to favor the prepared mind (with apologies to Louis Pasteur), your focus must be on preparing your mind for growth.

TECHNICAL VERSUS ADAPTIVE APPROACHES

For many years now, the state of the art in developing leadership talent has focused on what has been called "competency development." Competencies became the byword for all things about leadership development, and this approach has spun out an entire consulting industry. Competency development was (and still is) performed in a very targeted manner by focusing on identifying and "improving" specific, company-centered behavior patterns within individual leaders, regardless of whether these new behaviors have any resonance with the individual leader. This approach falls into the category of what Ron Heifetz from the John. F. Kennedy School of Government referred to as solving a "technical problem."

Heifetz differentiates between *technical* problems and solutions, and *adaptive* problems and solutions.[1] Technical problems involve very specific, limited, and identifiable challenges and have very limited, identifiable, and direct solutions. Adaptive problems, on the other hand, involve looking at complex phenomena and require long-term adjustments to fundamental aspects of the situation.

Heifetz uses the example of high blood pressure. There are two approaches you can take to resolve this problem. Solving it as a technical problem may involve taking medication regularly to lower your blood pressure. This provides a direct solution, addresses the problem directly, and can in the short term improve the situation. Alternatively, high blood pressure can be addressed as an adaptive problem. In this case, you may look to adjust your lifestyle—changing your eating habits, increasing your physical activity, and reducing your stress level. Addressing high blood pressure as an adaptive problem is more difficult, involves "growing" who you are as a person, and requires making changes across several areas of your lifestyle. This solution, however, also brings long-term benefits and substantial continuous improvement in your health.

Now let's look at how such solutions relate to leadership. Colin's real-life example shows him trying to fix a problem by using a technical solution. Let's look, instead, at how Colin might apply an adaptive solution. We begin by recognizing that there is a problem with others' perceptions about Colin's approachability. Our advice to Colin would be that he start by looking at areas of his performance where he is effective and productive. For example, we noticed that when Colin took on a task, he was extremely passionate about it and had a talent for seeing details that often escaped others. He was able to connect the dots faster than the others and pick holes and see around corners. In short, Colin had a real eye for detail.

One of the reasons people saw Colin as less than fully approachable was that he listened to them extraordinarily intently—he was utterly wrapped up in the details of what they were saying. So Colin needed to become aware of his CABs during those conversations. Instead of just focusing his attention on the content he was receiving, he had to expand that attention to the person who was in conversation with him in a way that was uniquely authentic to him. As he started doing that more, Colin began to change others' perceptions and they started seeing him as interested and committed. No one had to "fix" Colin's problem of lack of approachability; the problem corrected itself as Colin learned to adapt his CABs. Developing approachability for Colin was not about "walking the talk" or other such slogans, but about taking what he did well—focusing on detail—and expanding that to include the person as well as the task. That is authentic growth!

LIGHTBULBS AND LIGHTNING BOLTS

It is time for a small thought experiment. This will require you to picture four different things and describe them.

1. Picture a lightbulb. Describe it. What words come to mind? Bright, illuminating, useful, controllable, predictable, boring?
2. Now picture a lightning bolt. What words come to mind now? Bright, illuminating, powerful, dangerous, unpredictable, exciting?
3. Think of the last time you were in a classroom of any sort. This could have been in school, at a corporate training event, or in front of a computer for online training. Describe the experience. Are the words you used more like those used for a lightbulb or a lightning bolt?
4. Finally, picture the last time you took on an assignment where you had no idea how to begin or how to succeed. Describe it. Was it more like a lightbulb or a lightning bolt?

Reconciling the learning impact of an experience versus controlling the content of learning has been the dilemma facing leadership development for more than half a century. Trying to help people become leaders by placing them in a classroom has some distinct advantages—the time is focused, you know what the expected outcomes are, and you can create awareness and even inspire people. Also, no one gets fired, so it's a great safe environment. However—and it's a very big however—no one really learns to be a leader that way.

On the other hand, put people through the crucible of a career-making experience, and they will certainly learn an approach to leadership. However—and again, it's a big however—you have no idea what type of leadership they are learning. And sometimes people fail and get fired.

In a series of research experiments performed in the 1970s, the influential psychologist Albert Bandura demonstrated two important things. First, he discovered what was so eloquently stated by the great wit Yogi Berra: "You can observe a lot just by watching." The second thing Bandura discovered is that, while observing can teach you something, the knowledge does not become part of you unless you use it successfully in real circumstances. This led to an approach that we call "learn–then do," a combination of learning in the classroom, followed by attempting the practice in "real life," then getting feed-back. Seems a lot like a lightbulb.

The Problem with Muscle Memory

Martin Seligman applied the physiological concepts of *tonic* (muscles at rest) states and *phasic* (muscles in action) states to explain why it's so difficult to predict performance.[2] According to Seligman, just as measures of electrical impulses in muscles are not directly relatable from their resting state to their in-motion state, assessments of behavior and performance made in a "tonic" state—such as tests, interviews, or classroom have only a limited relationship to behavior and performance in a "phasic" state—when the person is actually engaged in performance.

Similarly, learning and development in the lightbulb or "learn then do" mode has a limited utility. In this mode we tend to develop automatic scripts—muscle memory—that we fall back into mindlessly every time we are faced with a situation or problem that we believe we have dealt with before. Leaders are encouraged to follow these steps whenever they recognize the situation. This is the essence of the athlete's motto, "Don't think, react." This approach to development seeks to create leadership muscle memory, with leaders reacting to situations with common, predetermined, preapproved behavior patterns.

We find there are two significant challenges with this approach. First of all, life is much more diverse and unpredictable than the events that arise on a football field or a tennis court. Although the number of situations confronting a leader may be diverse, as behavior patterns become more ingrained and automatic, it can become difficult for a leader to recognize nuances in situations where the old patterns do not apply. Worse still, relying on rote patterns of behavior encourages a lack of adaptation and flexibility.

Secondly, this approach encourages leaders to adopt behavior patterns that have been created outside themselves, as was the case with Colin. These behaviors may or may not be consistent with the way the leader sees himself and with who he really is. Inauthentic behavior patterns can be difficult to sustain, create barriers to relationships, and cause stress in the person trying to maintain an approach that she does not see as "hers." All of this may further lead to cynicism, frustration, and a lack of effectiveness.

As we have discussed, authenticity is critical to sustaining an approach over the long term. Rather than trying to grow as a Social Leader by adopting a number of automatic responses to specified situations, expand your portfolio of productive conversations, actions, and behaviors (CABs). These expanded CABs need to be both consistent with who you are as a person and engage the range of activities required to lead in the Social Age.

At this stage we need a lens through which we can focus on our effective and productive CABs: this is the lens we gave you earlier in the Tenets of Social Leadership. Each of the five tenets provides the space and channel to grow your CABs.

- Being mindful
- Proactively influencing the world around you
- Authentically relating to others
- Being open to new information and adjusting perspective
- Adjusting approaches for different audiences—social scalability

Growing these productive capabilities requires an approach that is personally meaningful, insightful, and focuses on development that is unique to you. We find that, rather than a "learn–then do" approach, this requires a "learn–while doing" approach. But remember not to confuse the "learn–while doing" approach with the "do then hope" approach, where you jump into a situation striving for success (or just survival) and retrospectively try to extract meaning! In the learn–while-doing approach, you take on new, challenging situations with a growth intent. We will explore this approach by discussing ways of turning lightning bolt experiences from do-then-hope moments to learn-while-doing opportunities.

SEMINAL EXPERIENCES

As we discussed in the last chapter, "seminal situations" render our normal way of responding insufficient. New challenges confront us and we find ourselves in deeply unfamiliar waters. Seminal situations involve four features: they are novel, are energizing, allow for "behavior innovation," and give us feedback on success and failure in the moment.

1. Novel. Novelty is the experience of being suddenly thrust into a situation that demands mindfulness. Our automatic ways of behaving, our "mind-less" patterns of reacting, are simply insufficient to deal with the situation at hand. We find ourselves struggling at first to understand the nature of the challenge and are even at a loss as to how to proceed. Novelty may arise from changes to:

- Content—the substance of the challenge; dealing with a challenge in a new functional area, for example
- Context—where the experience is occurring; dealing with a new region, location, or department
- Scope/volume—a significant increase in the range of impact of the challenge we are facing

2. Energizing. Seminal situations fully and deeply engage our interest, our excitement level, and our passions. These are situations in which we find ourselves struggling but motivated by the struggle. Something meaningful is at stake.

3. Allow behavior innovation. Seminal situations are those in which the proper path is not laid out before us. There is no best practice playbook to open up and there is no script to be followed. Others may have walked this road before us, but we are required to walk it in our own way, inventing as we go along.

4. Give feedback on success and failure. We win, we lose, we make progress, then we lose ground again; all of these may occur as we work to resolve the challenges of this seminal situation. True seminal situations are those in which we are able to gain feedback on the success and failure of our CABs. Sometimes our ability to gain feedback is inherent in the situation, and other times we must work hard to set up opportunities for feedback. Either way, feedback allows for the constant course correction necessary to understand which of our innovative actions are moving us forward to address these novel challenges.

THE LIGHTNING BOLT

Ever since Morgan McCall and Michael Lombardo published their critical study *Lessons of Experience*,[3] the power of developing leaders through direct experience has been recognized and seen as essential. We know how to set up seminal situations: significantly change either the content of what a leader is doing, the context in which he is doing it, or his scope of responsibility. Or perhaps change two or all three of these. Limit the constraints on what he can do to succeed. Ensure there is something real at stake and be sure he will know if he is succeeding along the way. We have been throwing people into the deep end of the pool for many generations. The ones who don't drown seem to come out better. Is that all there is to it? Not really.

These types of experiences are certainly seminal experiences as they contain all of the characteristics of seminal experiences we have previously discussed. These experiences are truly lightning bolts: bright, illuminating, exciting, and powerful...also dangerous and unpredictable. Recall the last time you were in a situation like this. As likely as not, you were in survival mode, doing whatever seemed best to survive the challenge and come through to the other side.

Do you learn from this? Certainly, yes. Do you grow as a result? Sure—just ask the dozens of people to whom you have told your heroic story over and over. But what did you learn and how did you grow? You may never fully know. In some respects, you will have grown the productive ways in which you lead. Maybe some approaches were so idiosyncratic to surviving that experience that you are likely to fail whenever you resort to them in other situations. And some of the CABs you leaned on to survive that experience may have proven destructive everywhere else. We refer to these situations as *thought-less* seminal experiences.

We suggest an alternative approach, which we refer to as *thought-full* seminal development. Have a look at the chart below.

Development Activity		Mind-set	
Thought–full seminal experience		Mind-set 3 –AUTHENTIC	Growth and change oriented
Structured training or structured experience		Mind-set 2 –LOGICAL	Openness or process oriented
Thought–less seminal experience		Mind-set 1 –REACTIVE	Survival oriented

FIGURE 5-1   Development Mind-Set

Mind-set 1 represents a thought-less seminal experience in which the individual operates in a reactive mode with the primary task of survival. It is a lightning bolt experience that will change the leader—but how much of the change will be productive is an open question.

Mind-set 2 represents a structured experience with a logical mind-set, allowing you to "master for the moment" a very specific set of behaviors in a controlled stable environment. Very much a lightbulb experience, it treats leadership as a technical problem. Will the specific behavior patterns imparted help you grow as a leader? It depends on the extent to which the behavior patterns you are being exposed to align with your authentic self and with the Tenets of Social Leadership. Will this be productive? Once again, it will depend upon how rigid your muscle memory tends to become. Will you be able to remain mindful and recognize when innovation is needed? We don't know.

Let's now look at the third way, what we call thought-full seminal experiences, represented by Mind-set 3. In these experiences, the individual approaches the challenge with a learning mind-set and an expectation of growth and change.

Thought-Full Seminal Experiences

Thought-full seminal experiences begin with three things:

1. Self-awareness
2. A seminal situation
3. Purposeful intent

Self-awareness involves knowing and owning your productive and unproductive aspects of the Social Leadership tenets and the CABs these lead you to undertake. In the previous chapter we discussed tools and approaches that will help you understand yourself as a Social Leader—use these tools to cultivate your approach in relation to the five Tenets of Social Leadership and recognize which of your CABs are productive, which are not, and why.

Seminal situations, as we discussed earlier, involve novelty (usually in the form of changes to the content, context, or scope that the leader is dealing with), emotional engagement (the leader cares about what is at stake), opportunity for innovation, and inherent feedback. Not every significant experience leads to a seminal situation. Some experiences require effort so that they become seminal, while others are important events but not seminal situations. When a significant event does occur, for example a promotion, relocation, or the need to clean up after a major failure, ask yourself the questions below.

Phasic Characteristic	Questions
Novelty	• Have I seen this before?
	• Why is this different from what I am used to?
	• How much of what I know can I apply here?

(Continued)

Phasic Characteristic	Questions
Innovation	• Is there a playbook for this situation? • Are there rules to be followed? • What restrictions will I face? • Who gets a say in the strategy for how I address this?
Emotional Engagement	• What is at stake for me? For the company? • Do I care? Why? • Am I excited, afraid, or both? • What happens if I do not succeed?
Inherent Feedback	• What does winning look like? • How will I figure out if I am on track? • What sources will there be for feedback? • How much do I trust them?

Use the answers to these questions to either enhance the situation, bringing it to the level of a seminal situation (one with real developmental possibilities), or to decide that this is a situation with limited developmental possibilities. For example, you may find that you need to negotiate a wider field of possible actions or identify a few trusted people from whom you can gather feedback along the way. Alternatively, if you truly do not care about the outcome of a situation, it is unlikely that it will impact you in a meaningful way.

Purposeful Intent

Purposeful intent refers to deciding early on that this challenge/event/opportunity in front of you is one you will use to expand your leadership capabilities. Once you make that decision you will engage in two actions, based on the Social Leader Learning Arc. The first involves setting up the conditions to create a learn-while-doing leadership growth opportunity out of the situation. The second involves creating a mindful intent to learn. We will discuss how to use the Social Leader Learning Arc to do both.

SEMINAL EXPERIENCES IN APPLICATION

In the previous chapter we introduced the idea of the Social Leader Learning Arc based on Joseph Campbell's hero's journey.[4] Here we will revisit this Learning Arc and use it as a tool to set up thought-full seminal development experiences.

The Social Leader Learning Arc

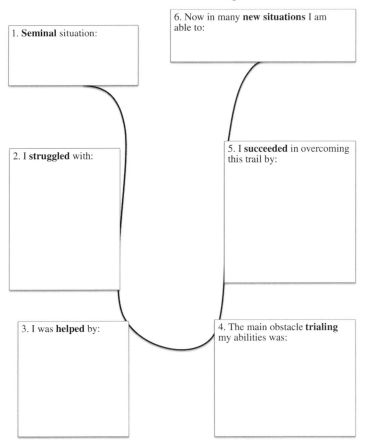

FIGURE 5-2 Learning Arc Icon

If you remember, we used the map above to help chart your learning from past experiences.

In this way, we treated past seminal experiences as thought-less development experiences, assuming that there was no development

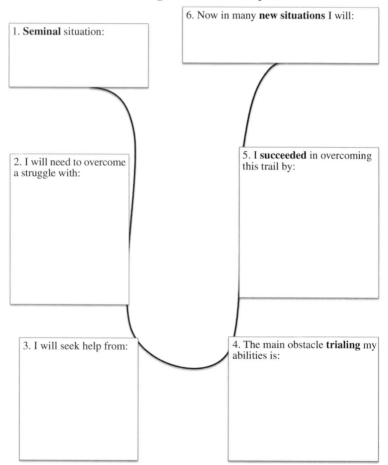

The Social Leader Learning Arc
Learning From Present Experience

6. Now in many **new situations** I will:

1. **Seminal** situation:

2. I will need to overcome a struggle with:

5. **I succeeded** in overcoming this trail by:

3. I will seek help from:

4. The main obstacle **trialing** my abilities is:

FIGURE 5-3 Prospective Learning Arc

cs.me

intent and that the results of these life experiences helped to build your repertoire of both productive and nonproductive conversations, actions, and behaviors. Essentially, we suggested using the Social Leader Learning Arc to examine past seminal situations to extract meaning. Learning your characteristic CABs help you make judgments about which are productive and which are nonproductive.

We now introduce a few changes to this map to turn it into a proactive development tool. Have a look at the Social Leader Learning Arc on the previous page.

Addressing the first three items in this map: situation, major obstacle, and sources of help are part of creating growth intent. These are the questions to answer before jumping into the situation. The table that follows lays out the questions to ask in order to be mind-full about what you are stepping into. Note that these questions presuppose self-awareness, that is, they assume you have a good understanding of yourself as a Social Leader. Having thought about the productive and nonproductive CABs that are part of your repertoire within the Tenets of Social Leadership will enable you to ask and answer these questions honestly.

Why is this a seminal situation?	• Why is this opportunity novel?
	• Is there a change in what I am doing, where I am doing it, or the scope I am impacting?
	• To what extent have I seen this before and, more importantly, in what ways is this different than what I have encountered before?
	• Why is this energizing?
	• What is at stake?
	• How important is it to me? To others I care about?
	• Do I really care about success here? Why?
	• Can I innovate?
	• What are the limits that are placed on me?
	• What constraints do I face?

(Continued)

	• Are these limits placed on me by others or by myself? Are they real?
	• Do I have the freedom to be unconventional in this situation? Why, why not?
	• How will I know I am succeeding?
	• What are the measurements that count?
	• Who is the judge?
	• Is there anyone I trust who is in a position to provide a sounding board, early warning signs, and honest feedback?
What is the major challenge and why will I struggle with it?	• What does success look like?
	• Why have others failed at this?
	• What are potential paths to success?
	• How will success be judged? By me? By others?
	• What don't I know about this situation?
	• What do I think I know but need to confirm? Why do I think this will be hard?
	• Which of my productive CABs can I lean on?
	• Which of my Social Leader tenets will be most tested, and which most need to be expanded?
	• Which unproductive CABs will I need to compensate for?
Where will I find help?	• Who is rooting for my success?
	• Who has addressed similar challenges?
	• What resources will I need and what can I do to make them available?
	• Who can I bring into the situation to help compensate for nonproductive CABs that may be critical to success?
	• Who do I see as possessing skills or CABs that I need to expand to succeed at this challenge?

Answering these questions will help you enter into this seminal situation prepared to grow, with some early pointers on assistance and support. This is the planning portion of a thought-full seminal experience. Taking action on these three parts of the Social Leader Learning Arc enable, but do not create, the learn-while-doing experience you are trying to establish.

Once you have considered these elements of the Learning Arc, it is time for mindful engagement. While you work to overcome the main challenge of the seminal situation, you will need to actively and regularly engage in the next two steps of the Learning Arc, which require that you consider these questions:

1. What challenges or obstacles are putting my abilities to the test?
2. How am I succeeding?

MINDFUL DEVELOPMENT: UNDERSTANDING LEADERSHIP TRIALS

Seminal situations, as we have noted, are defined in part by the need for "behavior innovation." Behavior innovation means having conversations, taking actions (making decisions and setting policy or strategy), and using behaviors that are not normally part of your comfort zone. These new CABs are required because the overarching challenge of the seminal situation and the smaller challenges along the way—leadership trials—will be those you have either not seen or not successfully confronted before. Approaching these trials with a growth intent means that you are striving to remain mindful in the situation—diagnosing what is going on, while it is going on.

When you find that you are struggling to lead successfully—that is, to influence and direct the attention and effort of others—look at the situation through the lens of Social Leadership. Keep the diagnostic questions that follow in mind as you determine within which tenet you need to innovate.

Mindfulness	• Am I reacting to what is going on at this moment, or am I reacting to something that has gone on in the past or might happen in the future?
	• Am I concerned about harming my relationship(s)? Am I concerned about becoming too close?
	• Am I looking at this situation from all possible angles? How do I know?
	• Am I looking out beyond the immediate situation?
	• What weak signals have I noted? What am I doing about them?
Proactivity	• What am I doing to drive this situation? What can I do to be more actively in control?
	• What am I doing that is reactive rather than proactive? How can I regain the initiative?
	• If I cannot control the circumstances, how can I better control my reactions?
	• Am I concerned about losing control? Being too much in control?
Authenticity	• How have I fully communicated the course of action I intend to take and want others to take?
	• What are my own motives? What is most important to me personally right now?
	• What am I doing to show those I am trying to lead I have their best interests and the best interests of the company at heart? Is it working?
	• Do they believe my take on the situation?
	• What am I doing to provide enough information for others to properly judge my actions?
Openness	• How fixed is my assessment of the situation and required actions? Why am I so certain?
	• What assumptions am I making?
	• Am I truly listening? Do others believe I am listening? How do I know?

	• What reactions are my CABs generating in those I am trying to lead? • What do I think those I am trying to lead are feeling and thinking about this situation?

Social Scalability	• How have I conveyed the importance and necessity of where I am trying to lead:
	  ○ In a way that is engaging to the entire group (organization, department)?
	  ○ To the team members in a way that lets then see themselves as a potent team?
	  ○ To each individual in a way that is meaningful to that person?
	• What are the stories others are telling about the CABs I have used in this situation? Are they helping to establish social energy?

Keeping these questions in mind will help you see where your leadership strengths are having a positive effect. Hopefully, after using the tools in the previous chapter to understand yourself as a Social Leader, little of this will come as a surprise. Using these questions to be mindful about your success as it is occurring will also provide clues to areas of leadership in which you are not being productive. Look at the areas you believe are limiting your effectiveness and consider which CABs you are using within that tenet. Now is the opportunity for innovation.

Take a hard look at the CABs you normally rely on within this tenet and which you are using in this situation, then take three actions. First, go to the sources of feedback you set up during the "help" planning, and confirm (or expand) your assessment. Do this in real time, while the situation is unfolding and you are asking yourself the questions above. New York City's successful and popular mayor in the 1980s, Ed Koch, was famous for constantly asking the question, "How'm I doin'?" That approach helped him earn three terms as mayor and have a bridge named after him.

Second, consider alternative CABs that can be used to compensate for the lack of success in this situation.

- Use the self-assessment work you have already done and consider again the list of productive and nonproductive CABs in the appendix.
- Look carefully at the chapters that follow in part 2 that deal with the tenets in which you are not productive to learn how to expand your productive capabilities in these areas.
- Reach out to some of the resources you planned for in the "help" step of the Learning Arc.

Before engaging in these new CABs, take a moment to decide if they really are authentically you. These may be approaches you have not tried or even thought about trying before, and that's fine. In fact, it is the whole point of behavior innovation.

The real question is, are these new CABs consistent with who you believe you are and how you see yourself? Or are they recommendations from others that fit more with their approach than yours? If it is the latter, it will be difficult to sustain them over time and, worse, may erode others' perception of you as authentic. Remember, compensating for a nonproductive area of your leadership with a strength is much more likely to succeed than attempting to "correct" this nonproductive aspect with CABs that are simply not you. Finally, remember that, at times, compensating for a nonproductive area of your leadership can mean bringing into the picture someone else to take on those CABs for you.

Finally, it is time for step 6 of the Social Leader Learning Arc: "*In many new situations I now will...*" This is the time for reflection about what you might do differently. Once the seminal experience has wound down, it is time to look forward and consolidate the changes and growth in leadership productivity you have made. Approaching this experience thoughtfully with a growth intent and working through the steps of the Social Leader Learning Arc will give you a solid understanding of the CABs in each of the Tenets of Social Leadership that helped you successfully navigate the challenges you faced.

The task now is to examine these CABs and identify the aspects of the situation that made these successful.

Rather than focus on the specifics of this situation, generalize the pattern within the situation that leads you to this specific CAB. For example, you may have found that three key players needed to work together as a team for the first time in order for the project to be successful. While ignoring this at first, you realized that you could rely on some of the CABs you use to create affiliation with individuals and scale them for a team to create needed cohesion. Generalizing beyond this specific situation, you now have some experience with the CABs needed to create relationships among a team, and these can be used whenever you see the need for tighter cohesion. Going forward, you may be more attuned to seeing cases where team cohesion is needed.

Once you recognize the new CABs that have proved effective and the patterns within a situation that make them relevant, you can answer the last question in the Social Leader Learning Arc and begin to extend your leadership capabilities. This approach to development through thought-full seminal experiences is one to be repeated over and over again as you grow as a Social Leader. It starts by being aware of your leadership capabilities, seeking out seminal situations, approaching them with a growth intent, and then working to authentically extend your productive CABs within this situation and planning to generalize them beyond this situation.

IN SUMMARY

We refer to development as becoming more. Rather than create new capabilities where none exist, we recommend instead that you grow the productive capabilities you possess and expand the situations in which you apply them. This journey begins, of course, with knowing yourself in relationship to the Tenets of Social Leadership. True development comes from balancing lightbulb experiences—focused and planned, with lightning bolt experiences—engaging and meaningful. We call these types of experiences thought-full seminal experiences. This chapter has provided a guide to help you identify and/

or create thought-full seminal experiences to aid your growth. Further, the Social Leader Learning Arc that you used to document past experiences in chapter 4 can also be used to help get the most out of thought-full seminal experiences. As you approach your own development, it is crucial to consider the mindset that you bring to the effort. An "authentic mindset" is one that begins with the intention to use an experience to grow, and an openness to rethink the conversations, actions, and behaviors you reach for to address different challenges. Bringing this mindset to a seminal experience is a powerful "learn while doing approach."

SUMMARY OF PART 1:
"CAN I GET THIS ON ONE PAGE?"

In a world where newspapers have become blogs, video has been shortened to Vine clips, letters have become instant messages, and opinions are expressed in 140-character tweets, our challenge as authors is to put this part of the book onto one page. Here we go.

The Social Age is here, replacing all that has come before. It is a world driven by socially created information, networked communities, and the prosumer. The new realities of this world are that knowledge is a commodity, the community is replacing the hierarchy as our primary organizing structure, and cheap communication and socially created information are accessible to all.

Along with all of the amazing benefits of this Social Age come a number of challenges, including:

- Constant disruption from difficult-to-forecast events
- The need to remain proactive in the face of ambiguity created by complex events born of independent, intertwined, emergent forces
- A change in audience; the community—composed of networks tied together through interest and passion—has become the defining unit to be addressed
- Information and meaning created constantly, communally, and in real time
- Easy access to global communication, which has given everyone a megaphone and made the crowd the editor of mass-distributed content

These challenges transform the work of leadership; rather than creating meaning and control, leadership now means harnessing Social Energy. We call this Social Leadership, and it demands that you think of yourself more like a mayor than as a general.

Social Leadership is not defined by a list of traits or characteristics. Rather it is a lens through which to view the conversations, actions, and behaviors (CABs) that are authentically part of the leader and are productive in harnessing Social Energy. We call this lens the Tenets of Social Leadership and there are five areas to explore, corresponding to the five challenges of the Social Age. The five Tenets of Social Leadership are:

- Mindfulness
- Proactivity
- Authenticity
- Openness
- Social scalability

Becoming a Social Leader is not about changing who you are. In fact, remaining true to yourself—being authentic—is crucial. Becoming a Social Leader is about becoming aware of your productive CABs within each of these five tenets and then expanding how you use them.

The process of developing oneself as a Social Leader involves understanding who you are in terms of these tenets—what we call your Personal Narrative—and then seeking out what we call having mindful seminal experiences. These experiences allow a learn-while-doing opportunity and need to be actively created and seized. We have provided a tool to assist with this process, called the Learning Arc, which offers a way to look at past experiences and uncover your Personal Narrative as well as a way to cultivate a growth mind-set for approaching current and future seminal experiences.

This summary is a bit more than one page but, like many leaders, we are immigrants to this new Social Age and are still learning.

Let's turn now to each of the challenges of the Social Age and look at how mayor–leaders use the Tenets of Social Leadership to address these challenges and at the conversations, actions, and behaviors that will be productive in addressing them.

Part II

The Social Leader In Action

In part 1 we discussed how the Social Age is upon us, driven by forces and defining features that stem from a world knit together by the complexities of global interdependence and cheap, massive, and distributed social communications infrastructure.

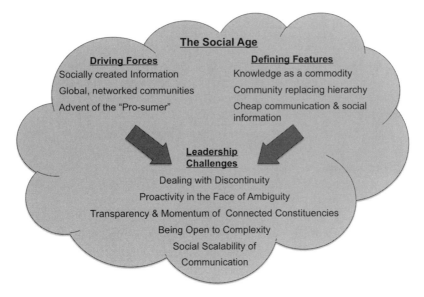

FIGURE Part 2 Social Age

This new Social Age has ushered in a shift in organizations; rather than being a traditional hierarchy, they are moving toward a flatter, community-based structure. At the same time, the leadership approach is shifting from that of a general to that of a mayor. Social Leadership is defined by five tenets that interact dynamically.

THE TENETS OF SOCIAL LEADERSHIP

In the following chapters, we'll explore each of the five key leadership challenges of the Social Age and the corresponding Tenets of Social Leadership. We will look at the productive conversations, actions, and behaviors (CABs) that Social Leaders can engage in to address these challenges.

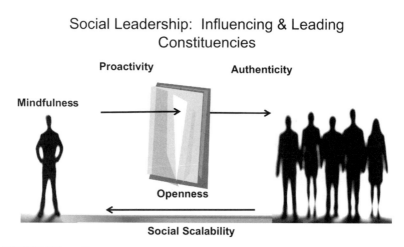

Social Leadership: Influencing & Leading Constituencies

Proactivity   Authenticity

Mindfulness

Openness

Social Scalability

FIGURE Part 2   Social Leader Tenets

As in the previous section, we will use stories and anecdotes from our research and experiences to illustrate the points we are making. In addition, we have written a case study that will unfold over these five chapters to more specifically illustrate the challenges of the Social Age and the productive and nonproductive CABs the leaders use in dealing with these challenges. Allow us to introduce you to IKU Industries.

IKU INDUSTRIES

IKU Industries is a manufacturer of custom design labels for use in clothing and other soft goods. The company provides labels and printing for major clothing manufacturers and boutique designers. The labels are used primarily on individual items. Recently, IKU Industries has moved into RFID labels, which allow individual items to be identified through passive scanners.

IKU has its headquarters in New York, with commercial offices in London, Milan, and Hong Kong. There are additional sales offices and distribution centers across the United States and Europe. IKU's main industrial design center is located in Bangalore, India, where there is also a new manufacturing facility. Fashion design is located in New York City and Milan, with R&D located in New York.

The privately held company had $1.2 billion in sales last year, with profits of $142 million and eight thousand employees. Half of IKU's employees have been added over the last four years. Originally, IKU Industries designed labels that were contract manufactured, at first in the U.S. and over the last fifteen years in China. At that time, the bulk of IKU employees were in sales, distribution, and design.

Four years ago, IKU opened a plant in India that manufactured machines to print labels directly onto cloth. This plant designs and creates programmable cloth-printing machines that are leased to clothing manufacturers. IKU designs labels, working with the brand owners' clothing designers, and programs its leased machines to print the custom labels.

Based on the experience it gained in cloth-printing press design, IKU moved into the development and production of RFID-embedded labels. RFID labels permit stores with RFID readers to quickly (and at a distance of up to two meters) read and identify items of clothing. This has reduced shoplifting, aided inventory control, and provided customer insights at the retail level. IKU owns the factory, located in Bangalore, that produces these labels. This facility opened a year ago, and sales of RFID-embedded labels are the fastest-growing segment of IKU's product line. All of these RFID labels are for individual retail products.

THE CRISIS

On a November morning in London, the team assembled: Tom Lee, the VP of sales and longest-tenured person on the team, Mary Hobbs, chief creative designer, Lisa Charles, VP of purchasing, and Gene Koss, recently hired VP of industrial design. Bob Roberts, EVP of Strategy, called the meeting to address a crisis the executive believes could threaten the very existence of the company. No one thought the meeting would be fun.

Everyone had coffee and some idle conversation as they waited for Gene to arrive, customarily fifteen minutes late. Bob Roberts began the meeting. "I think everyone is familiar with the situation, but let me go over the high-level points to be sure we are all on the same page," he said. "Over the last quarter, H&M, Walmart, and Inditex have approached all of their clothing suppliers and insisted that they incorporate smart labels into their retail-level items and their bulk packages and to link the two. All of our customers are now screaming at us about this. We think we have a year or less to deliver, or risk some serious account losses, maybe enough to threaten everything. At an emergency management committee meeting last week we decided to drive the needed changes through the company with a task force. You four are it."

The challenges facing IKU should by now seem familiar. The company is confronting significant business disruption from new technology that is impacting customers of their customers; IKU's leadership needs to be proactive without a clear understanding of the playing field; the transformation in front of them has the potential to change the very fabric of the company; and the need to be open and to communicate to both communities and individuals at once will become paramount.

As we look more deeply into what it means to be a Social Leader within a community-based organization we will revisit these four team members—Tom, Lisa, Gene, and Mary—and watch their story unfold. We will learn from their successes and missteps, and we'll use their conversations, actions, and behaviors as examples of the Tenets of Social Leadership. Let's take a look at the team's first meeting to get a sense of what they are up against.

THE FIRST CRISIS TEAM MEETING

Bob Roberts looked around the table at the four executives he was entrusting to lead this pivotal transformation effort and saw determination reflected back. Bob stood up and said, "Whatever you need, just let me know. This project has to be your top priority. When you are ready with a strategy, let me know and we will take it to the management committee." With that, Bob left the conference room. There was a moment of uneasy silence. Gene poured himself a cup of tea, sat down, and started texting.

"Well," Tom said, "we'd better start reaching out to see what the real requests are. I'll ask my people to start talking to their key accounts and try to get a handle on the actual needs and risks we're looking at."

Mary jumped in, "To me, the real issue is linking the tags from the retail items to shipping packages. What technical requirements will this place on our label designs? We need to know this. You can't expect our creative work to be limited by these new technical needs."

"Wait," sighed Lisa, "we don't even know what we are doing yet. How much will all this cost? What revenue can we expect? This might be really profitable and offset any loss from fashion design on retail labels. Let's try to get a plan together, set some timelines to develop a strategy, and still leave time for implementation."

"Look, I don't think we need to waste time on developing a plan for a plan," said Mary. "It's up to the four of us; let's set up a couple of meetings over the next few weeks, and I'll bet we can develop a way forward."

"Lisa's right about one thing, for sure," Tom laughed. "This could be really profitable. We may end up becoming primarily a logistics company, supplying smart bulk packages and getting almost completely out of our current business."

"Don't be ridiculous, Tom," said Mary, without a trace of a smile. "Once Gene gets the tech specs down we can get these package labels produced and they will simply be add-ons to what we are doing. Hey Gene, do you want to contribute here?"

Gene looked up from his smartphone. "I've been getting some of my engineers on this already. We are not the first people to be working on this. My guys think they can have the technical specs for this done in a month. I have one person already talking to plant operations so they are ready to cost out the production end and I asked HR to hire me a few people to expand our data mining end. This new business line should really help it take off. Tom, you should start talking to your customers about that." The room exploded. "What?!" Lisa almost could not make the words come out of her mouth. "Gene, you basically just told the entire company what we are thinking about without any plan at all."

"People are going to be pissed off, Gene," Tom said calmly. "Everyone is going to be wondering about what this means. There is already some tension between Bangalore and Hong Kong, and this is going to make it worse."

"Look, I am all for taking action and getting this behind us," chimed in Mary. "If Gene can get this done fast, have it only impact some parts of operations, let us continue with our core business, and give you more things to talk to customers about, Tom, what are we getting worked up about?"

"Mary," responded Tom, "first, I am not sure it is even up to us to approve this and get it going. I thought we were just supposed to make recommendations. Besides, Luther King [head of operations] is going to be furious that we are doing this without him. And how are we going to bring him into this now if he sees himself excluded?"

"We are going to need to look beyond ourselves, too, I think," continued Tom. "What does legal think? There must be privacy issues. What requirements do our customers have? We need to consider those." "Okay, okay," said Gene. "The task is in front of us and I am trying to get people focused on it and get it done. Isn't that what leadership is supposed to be?"

IKU is facing a moment of discontinuity. These moments, once so rare for us, have become commonplace. They are the crucibles within which productive leadership spells the difference between extraordinary success and living a life subject to the winds of the moment. We will follow these four characters as they face this crisis, learning from their mistakes and wins.

6

Dealing with Discontinuity: Leading from a State of Mindfulness

Do not dwell in the past, do not dream of the future, concentrate the mind on the present moment.

BUDDHA

TOM AND LISA MEET

Three weeks after their first meeting, Tom Lee, VP of sales, and Lisa Charles, VP of purchasing, decided that they would construct a plan for the new RFID effort and pitch it to the other team members. Tom had spent the intervening weeks talking to customers and anyone else he could about this new direction. Lisa had gathered information from her team on all of the relevant parts of the company that would be impacted—basically everyone—and tried to put it into perspective with the technical requirements that Gene Koss had his engineers work up. True to his word, Gene had delivered the specifications for what IKU would need to enter the bulk package smart label business within a month. True to his reputation, the specs were incomplete.

Lisa was already in the conference room when lunch and Tom arrived at the same time. "You certainly have your timing down," smiled Lisa. "I am glad we decided to get together on this. We may get more done, just the two of us. I have been working up a timeline and cost analysis for launching the new division, and I think this may be a very profitable new direction for us."

"Possibly," said Tom. "I am concerned about some things, though. Some of the people I have been speaking with are already starting to talk about what will come after RFID. Who knows, but we may be chasing something that has a short life span. And I think there is going to be some pressure on privacy issues. The latest government data-collection scandal has gotten everyone I talk to nervous."

Lisa tried to redirect Tom to the here and now. "Tom, we have customers responsible for 43 percent of our revenue insisting on these new package labels and, after investments, we could be profitable on this in eighteen months. The only real challenge I see is bringing Luther King from operations along. The last time we made a significant change and set up some production in Bangalore rather than Hong Kong he was furious, and was not at all cooperative. I am not sure where we will settle the new division, but Luther is likely to resist again."

"Well, Lisa, I remember that decision as being controversial and rushed. Over the last three weeks Luther has been in contact with Gene, and it seems all right. We should stay focused on this effort and not rehash the Bangalore project." Tom went on, "Still, I wonder if we should consider expanding this beyond textiles. If we really can develop bulk RFID label production cheaply with data ties to individual item labels, we might find a lot of new markets."

Lisa could feel her temperature rise. Tom's constant focus on getting every possible person on board was making her crazy. She thought to herself, "This will never get going if everyone needs to have a hand in it. Everyone will do their part once this is under way." Lisa knew she needed to calm down before going on, so she started to recheck some of the figures she had brought to the meeting.

Tom stared at Lisa for a full minute, waiting for a response, and then said, with a bit of a laugh, "Hello, Lisa? Are you still with me?"

Lisa snapped back from wherever her mind had gone and said, "Yes, Tom. I was just trying to think through the implications for the incomplete specs we got from Gene's team." In truth though, she could not recall what she had been thinking.

"Well," said Tom, "you're right of course about that, and possibly about Luther too. Let's go through all of the things you've put together and see what conclusion we come to. All I am asking is that we look over the horizon a bit."

"Fine," said Lisa. "Let's see how far we get and then we can share our thinking with Gene and Mary."

"Yes, and I've been wondering if there are others we should add to the team," said Tom. Lisa sighed and ate some of her salad.

AN AGE OF DISCONTINUITY

This Social Age is more than the intersection of social connectivity and seemingly limitless technological innovation. It is a time of continuous and recurring disruption to the competitive landscape. These disruptions are frequently called "discontinuities"—complete breaks in the expectations and trend lines we have relied on to create plans and guide actions.

Writing in 2008, Nassim Nicholas Taleb called these discontinuities "black swans," because historically such radical and unexpected departures from the norm were atypical.[1] However, Mike Canning and Eamonn Kelly of Deloitte Consulting, writing just five years later, made a rather different judgment: "Having recently concluded an analysis of the major trends reshaping commerce, we are convinced that the global business environment is experiencing major discontinuities..."[2] The business environment discontinuities we experience are driven not only by the forces of the Social Age but are compounded by the innovations our competitors—and, even more importantly, companies that formerly were not competitors—engage in to address the discontinuities they experience. According to Will Mitchell at Duke University, "Organizational innovation involves discontinuous changes in business practices."[3]

The traditional leader, in the role of general, takes up the tasks of creating plans, providing direction to the troops on achieving the objective at hand, and dealing with obstacles or variances that can be predicted. But how does a leader address the world of discontinuities—where objectives shift, where both the "troops" and the customers expect to be engaged in the conversation, and where obstacles are not only unpredictable but come from unpredictable sources?

The answer, of course, lies in acting less like a general and more like a mayor. The leader as mayor has a broad direction in which he is leading his constituencies but works at remaining mindful of the changes in the world around him—changes in the sentiments of his constituencies, the emergence of new competitors, and unexpected directions in which competitors are heading.

To Plan or Not to Plan

As we check in with two of our leaders from IKU, we see a tension that is often top of mind in leaders today: How much should we plan? In the previous case, Lisa is arguing to take the information at hand and create a plan with timetables, costs, and deadlines. Tom is arguing to stay loose, believing that the world will change twice before the plan comes to fruition and looking for "weak signals"—low-level information that may not seem relevant at the moment but could change everything in time.

Of course they are both right. You cannot move forward unless you know what you want to do and where you are going. However, in a world of frictionless information exchange, multifaceted connections, and rapid technological, social, and information advances—that is, a landscape of discontinuity—it is harder than ever to make long-term plans. As we examine the productive CABs Lisa and Tom use in this situation, we will recognize the mindfulness tenet.

Mindfulness as a term has been gaining in prominence and becoming increasingly associated with leadership rather than sixties-style counterculture. *The Economist* ran an article in November 2013 on what it called "The mindfulness business," catapulting the topic into the hallowed precincts of capitalism and market economics.[4] But while articles such as this tend to associate the growing importance of mindfulness with the stressful and nonstop environment of the corporate world, we take a different approach. We see mindfulness as a state necessary for addressing complexity and disruption.

To recap, we refer to mindfulness as a four-faceted awareness:

• **Temporal awareness**: being in the moment; for example, Tom looking at the current actions of his colleague Luther rather than at Luther's responses from the previous major project

- **Situational awareness**: reading the situation and forming an unbiased view of all possible impacts; for example, Lisa gathering information from across the company on the impact of the new strategy

- **Peripheral awareness**: understanding the potential impact *over the horizon*; for example, Tom talking to customers and others about their reactions to IKU's new strategy

- **Self-awareness**: appreciating one's own thoughts, emotions, and beliefs, and recognizing the impact of one's values on actions; for example, Lisa taking a moment before responding to Tom when she felt her anger rising

Physics of the Mind

Classical physics is the study of matter and its motion through space and time, and of related concepts such as energy and force. Analogously, mindfulness is an attempt to understand our perception of the world as it operates through time and space (awareness) and relates to energy and force (values). When a physicist wants to understand how and why a particle is behaving, she asks, "What is its motion (the time and space it occupies) and what forces are acting on it, with how much energy?" We are going to ask the same questions of ourselves to understand our own perceptions—to look at the way we interpret the world around us.

First, let's look at what we mean by perception. When we become aware of a conversation, action, or behavior (CAB) that has been originated by someone else, we interpret it. We try to understand what occurred, why it occurred, and what it means to us; then we respond. For example, imagine receiving the following e-mail from your boss: "I was wondering about the progress of your report—are things going well?" Did you just receive a show of concern, an expression of sympathy for being overworked, a reprimand, friendly encouragement, an expression of panic based on a looming deadline, or an attempt to remain tightly in control of the situation? Suppose you reply, "I have it covered, thanks." Did you just try to allay a concern, acknowledge a friendly gesture, tell your boss to back off, defend yourself from a reprimand, or create some space to work without your boss breathing down your neck? The answer depends on a combination of intention and interpretation.

How is this like physics? You may recall seeing a diagram in a high school textbook of a pool table and two balls, one moving and striking the other, which then moves. The physicist asks the question about where the two balls are and the forces are that are acting on each of them. With this knowledge the physicist can explain what happened and what the consequences of this interaction will be. We will be asking the same questions about CABs. For us, the person originating a CAB is the first ball in motion, which provides us with *intention*. The individual reacting to the CAB is the second ball, which moves in response to the first; here we will be looking at *interpretation*. The diagram below outlines this set of interactions in its simplest form.

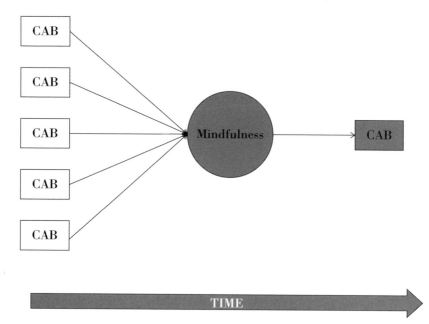

FIGURE 6-1 Mindfulness and CABs

Here we become *aware* of a number of CABs. We interpret these based on our own *values* and originate a CAB in response. Of course, the world is not that simple. In reality, the CABs that impact us look something like this:

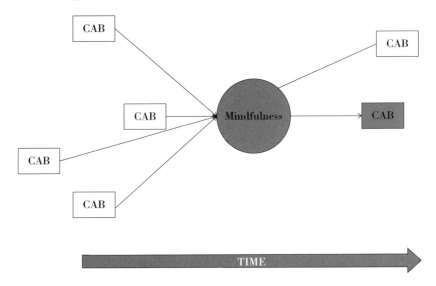

FIGURE 6-2 Mindfulness and CABs

Some of the CABs that influence us will be close to the point at which we take action and relevant to the matters at hand. Others will be on the periphery of our awareness, as they may not be directly or immediately relevant to the matters at hand. Some CABs will have occurred some time ago and may still be impacting us. Finally, some of the CABs that impact us may have not yet occurred—they are CABs we anticipate. How we react to this complex set of CABs is based on our interpretation of them. Our interpretation is in turn based on two things: the CABs of which we are selectively aware and the values we use to filter others' CABs.

Being aware of the CABs that impact us and the way we are impacted is how we portray mindfulness as an active aspect of leadership. Jeremy Hunter, from the Drucker School of Management, describes mindfulness as being present and aware of one's self, others, and the world; recognizing in real time one's own perceptions, biases, and emotional reactions; and realizing the actions one needs to take to address current realities effectively.[5] Mindfulness enables leaders to rapidly assess and respond to situations by stepping back into a zone of awareness, tuning in to what is happening, and watching and regulating their perceptions, thereby responding rather than reacting. Let's get back to the four-faceted nature of mindfulness:

- **Temporal awareness**—staying in the present moment
- **Situational awareness**—focusing on CABs that are directly relevant to the situation
- **Peripheral awareness**—tuning in to "weak signals[6]
- **Self-awareness**—understanding your own values

Let's look at each of these in turn.

TEMPORAL AWARENESS

There is a growing body of knowledge concerning the positive effects of mindfulness. The concept of mindfulness presented in this literature deals primarily with what we refer to here as temporal awareness, the aspect of mindfulness that involves being present in the moment and remaining in cognitive control. Temporal awareness is the antidote to *mindlessness*. Mindlessness is a common, pervasive, important but potentially destructive force.[7] When we act mindlessly, a common event triggers an automatic reaction. We are often not fully aware that we are reacting, because the whole process of perception–interpretation–reaction has become hardwired. It's a bit like driving a familiar route and not remembering the drive or eating a meal and not recalling putting the fork in your mouth. We see an example of this in our IKU case when Tom says to Lisa, "Hello, Lisa? Are you with me?" Lisa's mind began to wonder and she was no longer "in the moment" until she "woke up."

With all that we need to do in a day, autopilot can come in handy. These innocuous examples of mindlessness are geared toward conserving our energy so that we do not expend it on trivial tasks such as driving to the office. However, mindlessness can also become a habit, and its dangers are readily apparent. When we act mindlessly we act out of routine, disregarding new information and thereby making our habitual CABs unproductive. Acting mindlessly also means we are unlikely to recognize the novelty of a situation, and possibly may respond inappropriately or, more importantly, fail to learn from the situation. Finally, when we allow our brains to automatically select a response for us without our conscious control, we frequently act out of emotion rather than reason. Think back to a time when you have tried to deal with an unexpected disruption, and recall how easy it is for emotions to take over and hijack the brain's reasoning process.

For example, Hunter describes a series of experiments conducted by several other researchers in which individuals trained in temporal mindfulness are compared to untrained ones in a situation known as the Ultimatum Game.[8] In this game, two people—known as "the proposer" and "the responder"—are paired. There is a fixed sum of money and the proposer makes an offer to split the funds with the responder. If the responder accepts, each gets his respective share; if not, neither receives any funds. In the experiment, the "proposer" is always a confederate of the researcher and is told to offer an amount that is less than a fair share.

Logically, the responder should accept any offer that is above zero, with the understanding that something is better than nothing. However, only one in four responders accepted offers that were less than 20 percent of the available funds; all of the others refused such offers, feeling they were too unfair. These responders were unable to separate an emotional reaction to being treated unfairly from their behavior. The one in four who accepted the offer had been trained in mindfulness and was able to successfully regulate their negative emotional reactions. As Bill George, professor and former Medtronic CEO, observed in one of his *Harvard Business Review* blog posts, "The practice of mindfulness...teaches you to pay attention to the present moment, recognizing your feelings and emotions and keeping them under control...when you are mindful, you're aware of your presence and the ways you impact other people."[9]

Remaining in the moment helps to uncouple events from automatic emotional reactions based on the past. An example of this in the IKU case is the disagreement Tom and Lisa have over Luther's possible reaction. Lisa is anticipating a negative response from Luther based on his actions during a previous major transition in the company. Tom, however, draws Lisa's attention to the way Luther is reacting to this new project. While taking into account the history of past reactions is important, it is far more productive to deal with current responses. This is particularly true in the Social Age, when drawing trend lines and planning from past experience is more challenging than ever.

What can we do to avoid automatic, mindless CABs? Temporal awareness is itself a learned habit; it comes with practice. The habit of temporal awareness encompasses four elements:

1. Recognizing when your mind is on autopilot
2. "Seeing" your automatic thoughts and behaviors as if you were looking at someone else's
3. Bringing your attention back under your control and purposefully perceiving what is going on
4. Intentionally selecting a CAB

There are many classes and programs on mindfulness, almost all of which focus on what we call temporal awareness. While taking one of these classes is a fine activity, Hunter and his colleagues suggest a simple approach that we also endorse. Try to meditate each day, beginning with ten-minute periods and working up to twenty minutes.[10] To do this:

1. Set a timer so you are not worried about how long you are at it
2. Sit quietly and try to concentrate only on your breathing
3. When your mind wanders, and it will, do the following:
   a. Recognize that it has wandered
   b. "See" where it went—"What am I thinking about?"
   c. Return your attention to your breathing
   d. Be kind to yourself. Do not become frustrated, angry, or even disappointed that your mind wandered and you were

not able to maintain attention on breathing; your mind may wander a hundred-odd times in ten minutes when you first begin

4. When your timer goes off, stop and feel good about whatever success you have had

SITUATIONAL AWARENESS

Situational awareness is the second aspect of mindfulness. Here we are talking about being fully conscious of all the CABs that have direct influence on the matter at hand before selecting a particular CAB as a response. Seeing the whole field and responding to what is happening rather than reacting to what you *think* has happened is the core of situational awareness. In our IKU case we see Lisa using situational awareness when she reaches into all parts of the company to gather details on the impact the team's strategy will have on different parts of the company.

As we take in the world around us, we selectively perceive the CABs of others that we deem relevant and then interpret these CABs based on our own value system. We then produce CABs of our own based on this interpretation. Using this basic process as a foundation, improving our situational awareness requires that we do three things.

• **Remove the blinders.** First, we must become aware of the blinders we are using to select which CABs we attend. Blinders are a critical feature of our survival: without them, all that is going on around us would soon overwhelm us. Improving situational awareness requires that we have active rather than passive blinders. Passive blinders are those that we create out of habit or bias and use without thinking. For example, Nokia once owned the mobile phone market because of its outstanding telephone technology. This led to a reflexive blinder about the emerging importance of software and apps to smartphones, an error reminiscent of IBM's pass on an operating system known as DOS from a very small start-up called Microsoft.

• **Focus on the CAB, not perceived intention.** Secondly, improving situational awareness requires that we look at what *actually* happened rather than what we think was intended. Let's go back to the example we used to open this discussion. Your boss sends an e-mail inquiring about your progress on a report. It is easy to say, "My boss is pressing me on this report" or "My boss is worried about me," but the reality is, "My boss sent an e-mail asking about progress on the report." By focusing on the actual CAB, you can begin to put together an unbiased picture of the situation.

• **Suspend judgment.** There is a well-understood psychological principle that says once we form a judgment about something we tend to see new information as supporting that judgment and it takes an overwhelming amount of contradictory information for us to rethink our view.[11] So, tempting as it is, we can improve our situational awareness by working to hold off judgment until we gather as many actual CABs as possible. Consider forming working hypotheses rather than judgments, and continue to look for contradictory information.

PERIPHERAL AWARENESS

"Because that's what living is! The six inches right in front of your face!" A great Al Pacino line from the movie *Any Given Sunday*. Unfortunately, it's more complex than that. Figuring out what is relevant information amidst all of the weak signals around us is harder than it has ever been. Let's look at an example. The digital video recorder came into existence and the recording, storage, and retrieval of large volumes of televised programming became simple. For whom was this relevant? Every broadcast advertiser in the world, all of their advertising agencies, and all of the companies engaged in measuring media consumption understood this development as deeply relevant.

What about television writers? If you are a writer for a scripted

TV show, does this matter to you? Digital video recording would be an easy thing for a writer to ignore. Easy, that is, until the advent of binge watching, the phenomenon of fans hoarding multiple episodes or entire seasons of a TV show and watching them all at once. Suddenly, the structure of the shows you are writing needs to accommodate this new way of enjoying programs. Peripheral awareness is about seeing this change coming and paying attention to the CABs that do not directly influence what we are doing today but which have the capacity to change the nature of what we do in the future.

These currently not vital CABs are sometimes called weak signals.[12] In his aptly named book *The Signal and the Noise,*[13] Nate Silver describes the challenge of separating relevant information from a background of constant information. Trying to remain abreast of information that *might* be relevant at some future point compounds this challenge.

Cultivating a habit of curiosity is one of the best antidotes to peripheral blindness. Think about the course of your typical work-week: How many people outside your industry and profession do you speak with? What circle are you drawing your inputs and stimuli from? How many things do you read not directly relevant to your immediate activities? Increasing this number beyond zero is a first step in cultivating a habit of curiosity. In our IKU case we see Tom demonstrating this habit. His natural approach to gathering information on the proposed strategy is to go far afield outside of IKU and ask what others' reactions are both to the strategy he is considering and, more fundamentally, to the challenges he is trying to address. He is looking at what we call "adjacents."

Actively looking at adjacents is another way to improve peripheral awareness. Take a piece of paper, write your name and your current goal in the center, then surround this with the people, companies, constituencies, departments, and so on that directly impact your ability to succeed. Take the most important of these influencers and surround them with those entities that most impact them. These second-order influencers are your adjacents. How much do you know about them? Are you even sure you know who they all are? Set a plan to confirm that you have the right list of adjacents and then begin devoting some of your efforts to paying attention to what is going on with them. Your peripheral awareness will improve markedly.

SELF-AWARENESS

Self-awareness is essentially about becoming a witness to our own reactions. Looking at our IKU case, we see a classic productive CAB addressing self-awareness.

> Lisa could feel her temperature rise. Tom's constant focus on getting every possible person on board was making her crazy. She thought to herself, "This will never get going if everyone needs to have a hand in it. Everyone will do their part once this is under way." Lisa knew she needed to calm down a second before going on…

From a mindfulness perspective, self-awareness involves recognizing our own values and understanding where they come from and how they affect our CABs. Each of us holds a wide range of values relevant to different aspects of our lives. Here we are concerned with those values that affect our ability to succeed as leaders. More than five decades of leadership research[14] has shown that there are three internal drivers that play a large role in shaping the values we use in selecting CABs. These three drivers are: our need to *achieve*, our need for *affiliation* with others, and our need for *power*. Each of these is a bit more complicated than it seems on the surface. Let's look at them in turn.

"Fire in the belly," "Wants to win," "A real go-getter." It seems obvious. We look for this drive in the people we hire, we want to be seen this way, and this need for achievement is what should power a leader. Well, yes,…but not completely. Imagine a scale that runs from "It would be nice to win" to "I must win at all costs." We are all somewhere on this scale, and each point on the scale leads us toward the opportunity for both productive and unproductive CABs. Take a look at the chart that follows:

Extent to Which We Are Driven to Achieve	Productive Value Statement	Unproductive Value Statement
I must win, it means everything	*I will persist through difficult obstacles*	*If I fail, I need to figure out who or what (other than me) is to blame*
I want to win, it's important to me	*Let's be realistic about what we can achieve*	*Let's stay in our comfort zone*
I would like to win but it's okay if I don't	*Let's be open to others' agendas*	*Let's delay our goals until a more favorable time*

As you can see, there is not necessarily a "sweet spot" on this scale. The goal is to recognize that we will have biases when selecting CABs as well as in trying to interpret the CABs that we see. Let's go back to our example of the boss asking about a report status. If you are a *must win* person, you might interpret your boss's e-mail as meaning, *"Can I blame this person if the report is late?"* If you are a *want to win* type of person, you may interpret this e-mail as your boss saying, *"I need to know so I don't over commit on a deadline we might miss."* If you are a *would like to win* person, you may see this e-mail as your boss thinking, *"Let's renegotiate this deadline."* The same biases are in play when we select the CABs we use.

Let's look at our inclination to be liked and to be part of a group, what psychologists call our *need for affiliation*. Again, imagine a scale, this one running from *"I live and breathe relationships"* to *"I rely only on myself."* Now let's look at the chart below.

Extent to Which We Are Driven by Relationships	Productive Value Statement	Unproductive Value Statement
Maintaining good relationships is everything	*Let's find a way for everyone to contribute*	*Let's avoid direct confrontation*
I need others to succeed	*Let's get as many people on board as we can*	*If we get the right people on board, we can pressure the rest*
I rely mostly on myself	*Let's get some traction and others will get on board*	*If you are not with us you're against us*

Again, we can begin to see the potential biases that creep into the CABs we choose when we act without conscious attention to our own values. And again, there is no "sweet spot" on this scale, though the extremes tend to involve a higher number of nonproductive CABs. For a particular situation it may be crucial that everyone is connected, while in another situation it may be necessary, even preferable, to go it alone for a while. Unless you are actively aware of your values, preferences, and biases, it is easy to fall into a predictable pattern of CABs that fit with these values but may hinder your success in that situation.

Further, our need to maintain relationships affects how widely we think when considering whose agendas we care about. If you are less driven by relationships, it is possible that you take into consideration primarily your own agenda (and perhaps that of a close colleague) at the expense of your constituents' agendas. If you are moderately driven by relationships, you may focus on your team's agenda ahead of anything else, giving less attention to your own best interests or those of a broader set of constituents. If you are strongly driven by relationships, you may focus on creating broad consensus at the expense of maximizing success.

Finally, when looking at the drivers of our key leadership values, let us consider the very poorly named "need for power." The concept of our need for power, first articulated by psychologist Henry Murray,[15] actually refers to comfort with and preference for getting things done through others. Whereas a person with a high need for power walks into a room, sizes up a challenge, and begins assigning tasks to everyone around, the person with a low need for power is loath to do so. Think of the scale for this value as running from, *"Let me tell you what I need you to do"* to, *"If it isn't too much trouble, could you help me with this?"*

Consider the chart below.

Extent to Which We Are Comfortable Directing Others	Productive Value Statement	Unproductive Value Statement
I will orchestrate everyone involved in this effort	*Let's clarify roles and move quickly*	*I've got the answer, do it my way*
I will direct those I feel responsible for	*We are a well-oiled team that I keep on track*	*Those people are not my responsibility, I have no authority to give them direction*
I'm sure everyone knows what needs to be done	*Everyone here is talented and will deliver without my interference*	*Who I am to tell others what to do?*

As with the other internal drivers, there is no universal sweet spot on the scale. The extreme ends of the scale contain more opportunity for unproductive CABs, and if we are not aware of our values, we will select CABs that are in line with our preferences but which are not necessarily most productive in the situation.

It's critical to understand that all three of these internal values drivers—the need for power, for affiliation, and for achievement—are present within us at the same time, interacting to guide our choices.

So how do we remain self-aware? One solution is to recognize that acting in ways consistent with our values makes us feel comfortable, while acting in ways that are inconsistent will make us uncomfortable. You can take advantage of this by periodically asking yourself two questions: "How do I feel about what I am doing?" and "Why?"

If you are comfortable with the way you are addressing a challenge, you should be asking yourself: "Is this the most effective way to proceed or simply the one I always use? What might someone choose to do differently and how might that work out?" If you are feeling uncomfortable with your actions, ask yourself: "Am I acting inconsistently with my usual preferences? Why am I using these CABs? Am I acting productively but in a way that is new and stretching me, or am I acting in a way that is inconsistent with who I am because I am being pressured to do so?"

Once you become mindful of the role your value preferences play in the CABs you select, you can start choosing to act productively rather than out of habit. Brian Little, an award-winning scholar and teacher who has taught at Harvard and Cambridge, refers to this as "acting out of character." We may consciously choose to act out of character,[16] as when an introvert is able to act in an extroverted manner and then returns to her introverted preference.

One final note on self-awareness concerns authenticity. Our internal value preferences make us who we are, guide us toward CABs that are consistent with our self-image (who we strive to be), and allow others to understand how we may react in different circumstances. The goal in addressing the self-awareness aspect of mindfulness is not to change your value preferences. Rather, the goal is to become aware of them so that you can broaden the productive CABs you use and become aware of CABs you use automatically, even though they may not be productive in the given situation.

IN SUMMARY

In short, mindfulness is a core Tenet of Social Leadership that leaders use to help anticipate and react to disruption. Mindfulness involves four facets:

- Temporal awareness—am I "in the moment"?
- Situational awareness—am I conscious of everything that is relevant?
- Peripheral awareness—am I giving enough attention to weak signals (adjacents)?
- Self-awareness—am I acting purposefully or am I reacting out of my unconscious value preferences?

There are techniques to help us improve our ability to be more aware in each of these four areas:

- Temporal awareness—use meditation to regulate where you are placing your attention
- Situational awareness—remove blinders, focus on others' CABs rather than your interpretation of them, and suspend judgment for as long as possible
- Peripheral awareness—identify adjacents and set aside some energy to keep abreast of them
- Self-awareness—regularly check your comfort level and ask, "Why am I feeling comfortable/uncomfortable with my actions?"

7

Moving Through Ambiguity: Proactively Influencing the World Around You

I don't like that man. I must get to know him better.
ABRAHAM LINCOLN

GENE AND MARY MEET WITH THEIR TEAMS

The RFID crisis team, as they called themselves, met six times and fleshed out a clear path forward. There would be changes to almost every part of the company and rigorous cost cutting to balance out the expense of adding the new division. Tom had insisted they all take the plan back to their respective departments to see how everyone reacted. Of course, these meetings were more like town hall meetings than briefings, as everyone seemed to have already heard about the plan and formed an opinion. Someone had even started a "Got Bulk?" thread on IKU's internal blog.

Passions were running high across the board. When Mary e-mailed all of her senior designers to come to a meeting in Milan to discuss the plan, one responded by asking if the meeting should be in Hong Kong. Gene learned that the design engineers in Bangalore had started a job-lead sharing page on Renren, the popular Chinese social networking site.

Mary called her meeting to order and shared the outline of the plans for the new division with her senior designers. She said, "This is the best thinking we have come up with so far. Everyone involved is holding meetings like this to get a bigger perspective." Everyone already knew most of what was said but some of the details came as a surprise. "Mary, we have been talking about this for the last month among ourselves. In our view, the approach unnecessarily limits what we can do creatively. Here are five things we've come up with that can give us back some creative freedom and an ability to better respond to customer requests," said Gian Carlo, speaking for the group. "Look," said Mary, "I believe creativity should be at the heart of everything around here. I'll support anything that drives that home and also helps IKU succeed."

Mary looked at the list and realized two things: they were right about the changes they suggested and, since each of these items would change aspects of the plan that affected other departments, there was no way to know what the ripple effects would be. Mary looked up from the list and said, "If we are going to create these changes in the plan there are a number of things we need to do." She led a discussion on getting more detailed information on costs and process, and the group talked about how to connect with clients to ask for their input. Then she said, "We will need to move quickly. We can definitely influence the plan with these changes if we act now. Getting sales and industrial design on board will be critical. I can work with Tom Lee, but I don't speak engineering—who can take that one?"

When Gene arrived at his team meeting, everyone was a little cranky. The meeting was in Bangalore, where most of the industrial designers worked, and a number of the senior R&D staff from New York had flown over. Gene had postponed the meeting three times because some emergency had come up, and now he was twenty minutes late. He walked into the conference room and said, "Sorry, I had a call with someone from auditing and he just wouldn't let me off the phone. I've noticed you have all been busy chatting on this cute page on Renren, by the way. Let me lay out the plan for you." When he finished, Gene said, "As you can see, they took our design specs as the foundation for the plan so we should all be happy. The company will do a great job putting this in place."

Rakesh, the longest-tenured manager on the team, looked around and said, "Gene, we are all happy the company liked our ideas on the design for the new equipment. We think that the implementation could be better. We have some ideas we would like to share." Gene raised his hand, "Rakesh, I appreciate you and everyone here. But how our ideas get implemented is not our concern. What we need to do is listen to what we are asked for and then deliver it. We've done that and you all have done a fine job."

Rakesh continued, "Just a few changes, for example, in the sales data process and the way distribution centers are planned to operate might help us in the future."

"I take your point," said Gene, "but I cannot change the way those departments operate. We are the engineers, not the business planners. But I'll tell you what, send me an e-mail with your notes and I will send them around to the team. But don't get your hopes up. Now, just let me say again, good work on this, everyone." Rakesh sat down.

THE CHALLENGE OF AMBIGUITY: PARADOX 1

Whether 'tis nobler in the mind to suffer the slings and arrows of outrageous fortune or to take up arms against a sea of trouble . . . ?
WILLIAM SHAKESPEARE

If you want to lead, Hamlet, you don't have a choice. To be or not to be? To do or not to do? In our work, we have watched leaders struggle with this choice. And some have successfully waited on the sidelines for "strategic direction from above" and then "led their people to flawlessly execute" on the received strategy. This, of course, was General McClellan's approach during the American Civil War. While this tactic may have worked in the past, all we can say to those who attempt this today is, good luck. In a world where leaders were crucial linchpins in a downward flow of communications and strategies were set for long periods of time, this passive approach had an opportunity to succeed.

In today's networked world, where everyone has access to broad communication tools and can shape the conversation, standing on the sidelines is not a productive option for a leader. And yet simply defaulting to the activist general—Ulysses Grant, for example (in contrast to McClellan)—and shouting "troops, take that hill" is also a recipe for leadership failure. Aligning people with your point of view is possible but not always productive when passionate employees wish to be fully engaged in creating a communal point of view.

How does a productive mayor–leader take an active stand without alienating constituencies who expect to participate in setting direction and creating meaning? To be productive, the Social Leader must address the first paradox of succeeding within ambiguity: holding a values-driven point of view and influencing constituents to move toward this point of view *while* acknowledging the validity of other viewpoints. A leader does this by communicating his viewpoint as *a* point of view rather than *the* point of view.

Further, the troops no longer stand silently waiting for the general to speak: The mayor uses every moment to shape the cacophonous din of many constituents participating at once. Most importantly, the productive Social Leader believes that she is capable of influencing and harnessing these passions rather than being carried away by them. In this way, the Social Leader is an "actor in" rather than a "receiver of" socially created meaning.

To perform this balancing act, a Social Leader must be a *performative artist*; we will come back to this after we've discussed the second paradox.

THE CHALLENGE OF AMBIGUITY: PARADOX 2

David Levin, then CEO of UBM, needed to transform the company's business model away from print publications and into events and data analysis. The first step in this transformation was, as he described it, *"generating self-belief"* within the organization and the leadership. He did this with start-up projects in media, events, and data management. He worked to make sure that word spread about successes. This went a long way toward helping the community of employees believe that, not only could they succeed, they could shape and drive the direction of the transition.

Not only must a Social Leader have the self-belief to act, he must be willing to act in the face of imperfect understanding and incomplete information. That you will not have all the information before you act is today a given. More to the point, it is unlikely that, with the information you have, you will be able to form a definitive prediction about the near-future environment you will face.

A recent report by Duke Corporate Education titled *2013 CEO Study: Leading in Context* makes clear the challenge leaders face in taking action in today's interconnected, socially driven landscape: "These CEOs emphasized how difficult it is to lead effectively in a context where the shelf-life of information is unstable, the interconnection of information resources is non-linear, access to information is uncontrollable, and the source of true differentiation lies in figuring things out as opposed to finding things out."[2]

Rather than posing a solution to this challenge, the study's authors pose a provocative question for a leader: "How long can you hold on to multiple conflicting hypotheses about which course of action to take until you can see the way forward that gives you the most leverage?"[3]

This suggests a significant revision to the old metaphor of Tarzan swinging through the jungle on a vine; traditionally, if he is to move forward, Tarzan must let go of the vine he knows is stable and grab the next vine without assurance that the new vine will hold. In today's world, the challenge for Tarzan is to swing out on the first vine without knowing whether he will come to another vine; or if the jungle will transform into a sea instead, or into a city, and he will need to hail a cab instead of grabbing a vine. It is one thing to move from a stable vine to another vine without full assurance. It is another thing entirely to set out on a vine without being sure if your next move is to grab a vine or a boat or a cab.

How does the mayor–leader maintain the capacity for action amid an unpredictable competitive landscape? This brings us to the second of the two paradoxes: maintaining a clear sense of self-efficacy (a personal fact-based belief in your capability to succeed or, as

David Levin called it, self-belief) *while* being willing to live with ambiguity and move without complete understanding (or knowledge) of all of the forces, stakeholders, and contingencies that can affect your success. In short, keeping your sense of self-belief without knowing all of the answers.

The ability to hold together the paradox of self-efficacy amid ambiguity creates the context for a leader to be proactive. This means asserting and maintaining influence on the direction of events with:

- Multiple constituencies expecting a voice in setting direction
- An inability to control the flow of information
- An imperfect understanding of current influences and future events

PROACTIVITY

Addressing the challenge of ambiguity is the Tenet of Social Leadership we call Proactivity, the belief that one has the ability to initiate, execute, and control one's own actions in the world.[4]

In our case study of IKU Industries, Mary and Gene are bringing to their teams the plan for building a new division and transitioning the company. Immediately they are confronted with the realities of the Social Age:

- They were not in control of information—their departments were already aware of the plan, had formed an opinion, and had created responses while the leaders on the crisis team were talking among themselves
- The staff was not just talking among themselves but across the organization (and, in the case of the industrial designers, outside the company as well)
- Their people wanted very much to influence what was going on and expected to be able to do so
- Any action involved areas not within the leader's direct control, requiring influence and the blending of additional agendas

Looking at Mary and Gene, we see two contrasting styles. Mary took on the challenge of proactivity headfirst. She demonstrated in the conversation with her team the actions she was willing to take. And she demonstrated by her behavior that she saw it as her role to continually influence both the conversation and the execution of the plan across all constituencies. Gene, by contrast, took his meeting as an opportunity to inform his troops, praise them, and tell them to wait for orders from above.

Here is what their CABs look like through the lens of proactivity:

Proactivity	Mary the Mayor	Gene the General
Moving **without full understanding**	*"We will need to move quickly"* and . . . *there would be no way to know what the ripple effects would be*	*"What we need to do is listen to what we are asked for and then deliver it."*
Values-driven point of view	*"I'll support anything that drives that (creativity) home and also helps IKU succeed."*	*". . . they took our design specs as the foundation for the plan so we should all be happy."*
A point of view **not** *the* point of view	*"This is the best thinking we have come up with so far. Everyone involved is holding meetings like this to get a bigger perspective."*	*"Let me lay out the plan for you."*
Focus on **self-efficacy**	*"We can definitely influence the plan with these changes"* and *"I can work with Tom Lee but I don't speak engineering. Who can take that one?"*	*"I cannot change the way those departments operate. We are the engineers, not the business planners."*

Here we see Gene poised at the threshold of inaction. Caught up in linear logic of either/or, he has faith in the plan and in "the company" rather than in his own ability to influence events. As a leader he is working to define the space in which his department should operate and encourages his team to focus on these accountabilities, leaving everything outside the frame to others.

Mary, by contrast, has a strong sense of proactivity. Her actions and behaviors convey to her team that anything that drives their collective purpose is fair game. Notice that we said collective—not common—purpose. Mary does not seek to "align" her team to her plan. She is looking to them to shape the plan and interpret what is going on. She is clear about what she values and what she will support without insisting that others sign on to her values.

Earlier in the book we talked of Jonathan Donner, vice president of global learning and capability development at Unilever. Unilever, which began as a merger of English and Dutch companies, operated using a dual corporate structure with co-CEOs headquartered in both the Netherlands and the United Kingdom for nearly seventy years. In 2005, Unilever changed its management structure in favor of a single CEO and dramatically simplified the organization, moving to three divisions from eleven. These moves created a considerable amount of ambiguity and uncertainty throughout the organization. A critical approach to dealing with the transition was to pull the leadership around the world together to help forge the vision and direction of the renewed Unilever.

Jonathan was tasked with leveraging the fabled London-based training center known as "Four Acres" to accomplish this task. Over a five-year period Jonathan directed Four Acres to bring hundreds of senior executives from around the world together on world-class development programs with the active participation of the CEO and Board, to actively participate in the business vision, which was originally called "One Unilever" and later became "The Compass." As these visions matured, and with the appointment of a new CEO, this community of leaders increasingly cast their ambition towards developing and emerging markets, with a focus on Asia. Given the iconic status of Four Acres and its role in shaping Unilever's business, leadership culture, and talent, the decision was made to build a second Four Acres Leadership Centre in Singapore.

Based on a personal commitment to maintaining the concept, standards, and intent of Four Acres as it was translated to Asia and expanded globally, Jonathan requested a relocation to Singapore to complete the build process and lead the stabilization of its initial period of operation. "While we sought to build a second, magnificent Unilever learning site, I was acutely focused on creating the existing concept that respected the importance of how the content we delivered connected with the context we were creating. Creating meaningful content for participants and the business, while protecting the concept of Four Acres, I saw as critical to the Singapore center becoming a sustained success."

Jonathan's initial work involved directing architects and construction firms, bringing in renowned learning design experts, engaging in discussions and negotiations with government officials, and importantly, ensuring that the voices and needs of internal Unilever constituents were managed and represented. In June of 2013 the $40M-plus learning facility, recognized for its environmental design and spanning six acres, was opened by CEO Paul Polman and the Singapore Prime Minister. As we discussed this with Jonathan, he told us about the first groups he approached to attend Four Acres Programs in Singapore, which included global executives from the Americas, including Argentina.

A quick check of Google Earth will explain the confused looks we gave Jonathan. As he explained, putting a Four Acres center in Singapore would only have meaning if it served the same purpose as the center in the UK—ensuring the diversity by connecting executives around the world to join the conversation and influence the direction of the company. Putting a learning center in Singapore was a way to communicate the importance of Asia to the future of the company; having it only serve Asia while the UK center served the west would not be in line with the Four Acres mission to develop a global community of leaders. Since then, Jonathan has worked hard to defend and underline this logic in the face of travel budget cuts and continued challenges, as he sees this standard as vital to the long-term integrity of what Four Acres uniquely represents to Unilever.

We see in this example many of the same productive aspects of proactivity we saw in our fictitious leader Mary: a willingness to take action, even without a full understanding of all the contributing influences and potential outcomes, and actions based on values and a willingness to work with multiple points of view. We also see the breadth of constituencies a leader in the Social Age must address and the need to act beyond boundaries to maintain one's influence. Let's look at each aspect of proactivity in turn and explore the productive conversations, actions, and behaviors in which Social Leaders engage.

LEARNING TO BE A PERFORMATIVE ARTIST

We draw the term *performative artist* from the work of philosopher Jürgen Habermas, who coined the term *performative contradiction*.[5] A performative contradiction is a paradox in which the content of one's actions and the actions themselves contradict each other. For example, the statement "There is no such thing as truth" is a performative contradiction because the speaker is making a claim he believes is true but which states there is no such thing as truth. Other examples include creating a plan that encompasses the idea that it is impossible to predict the competitive landscape or asking everyone's input on a strategy that is already fixed.

Leading in our socially defined, discontinuous world means being able to remain credible (and sane) while creating and leading within performative contradictions. For example: "We must keep everyone engaged while we reduce head count 10 percent." How can you, the productive mayor–leader, make this statement and expect those around you to take you seriously? Answering that question takes us into the heart of performative artistry.

Values

The performative artist knows that being productive in the face of contradictions means understanding and living your values. In the example above, the Social Leader making the head count statement may have a strong belief that "making positive contributions at work is a way to maintain one's pride" and may have communicated that this is a core value for her. If that is the case, when she announces,

"We must keep everyone engaged while we reduce head count 10 percent," what everyone hears is, "I will help you maintain your pride even if you are affected by this reduction."

Of course, it will do you no good as a leader to suddenly "discover" your values at the moment they are needed. Try this: make a list of some of the most difficult decisions you have had to make. Recall what was behind each decision—on what did you place value? The list might seem a bit long at first. Now, for each item on the list ask yourself, "Would I walk away from my job if I were asked to violate this value?" Be honest and the list will get shorter quickly. Now you have your true core values. What do you do with them? You may want to try three things: always act with these values in mind, let others know that you are doing so, and hardest of all, remember that others hold values too, and their list may be different. This brings us to acknowledging the validity of other points of view.

Valuing Others' Points of View

If you have spent any moment in your life reading or thinking about philosophy (including that required freshman class) you may be aware that for centuries the debate has raged over whether logic and truth exist independently or only as part of our subjective points of view. The Social Leader learning to be a performative artist will have to suspend that debate, however interesting it is, and focus on one fact: every single day, we have conversations, take actions, and behave in ways that are characteristic of ourselves. All of these CABs are drawn from the way we see the world, and our vision of the world is strongly impacted by our values.

Other people also have a vision of the world, and their vision is strongly impacted by their own values, which may well be different from yours. Keeping this in mind and holding that contradiction together is what drives success as a performative artist. How can you do this? There are three steps:

1. Use CABs that clarify that you are acting from your values and that you recognize that others may have different values

2. Ask those around you how they see the situation—the contradiction—and decipher the relevant values they hold
3. Widen your field of vision so that your CAB takes into consideration the perspectives of your constituents

SELF-BELIEF

Recently, one of the authors of this book was working with Fabrizio Alcobe, SVP of Administration at Univision Networks. While driving to a meeting, Fabrizio explained that he was in the middle of a difficult negotiation with another senior manager. The negotiations were complex because a good many people were involved, not everyone was fully aware of all the aspects of the negotiations, and some very senior public figures were in danger of being embarrassed.

Fabrizio was concerned but confident he could handle the situation. As he explained, while working in a different company several years earlier he had learned that his boss was to be fired and that he would be involved in arranging the severance agreement with the board of directors. It was a real trial that tested his loyalty and forced him to deal with a shifting political landscape. Though the situation was personally painful, the executive learned that he was capable of identifying what information needed to be conveyed to whom and doing so with the discretion necessary to keep these sensitive activities on track while also maintaining his own sense of loyalty (a core value for him).

He carried this belief in himself, this efficacy for managing sensitive political situations, into his current role. This sense of self-efficacy allowed him to maintain an active role in these negotiations, directly and positively influencing both the specific details of the deal as well as the quality of the relationships with those involved. This self-belief was not a fanciful hope but a fact-based belief rooted in real experience. The term self-efficacy originated with one of the twentieth century's great psychologists, Albert Bandura.[6] Essentially, Bandura was referring to a person's fact-based belief that if he tries to accomplish a particular thing he will succeed (for example, leading a group through a crisis, remaking a company's business model, or carding par for a round of golf). Notice that we are talking about fact-based beliefs. Bandura was not suggesting a plot from a feel-good children's movie in which a group of poor-skilled ballplayers overcome their highly proficient rivals simply because they have heart and believe they can succeed. While this may be a great story line for Disney, it's an unproductive approach for a leader. Self-efficacy means looking at past successes and extrapolating to a current set of circumstances.

How can you develop this sense of self-efficacy? First, it is important to recognize that there is no true thing as *general self-efficacy*, that is, "I can achieve anything." True self-efficacy is rooted in a particular activity, for example, managing a complex political negotiation. Then it is about creating opportunities for yourself so that you develop a track record of success in an area. These opportunities need to be scaled in a way that you can both create success and recognize the CABs that led to this success.

Let's draw a lesson evident in the stories of both Fabrizio Alcobe and UBM's David Levin, who worked to build self-efficacy for business transition into his leadership team. Levin purposefully set up a number of test cases and small trial projects; our TV executive was thrown into a situation where he needed to be a part of terminating his boss. Importantly, though, he was a part of this process and not the key driver, and though a misstep might have hurt his career it was unlikely he would be in a position to make a catastrophic mistake.

Both of these stories show us the same pattern: a novel situation in which the stakes are real but manageable, ultimately ending in success (even if there were some setbacks along the way).

Also, the leaders in both these situations took the time to examine the CABs that made them successful and were able in the future to identify similar situations—where the stakes were much higher—so that they were confident in their ability to take action to handle these new, higher-pressure situations. This leaves us with three steps for building self-efficacy:

1. Make concerted efforts to have new experiences in which the consequences of failure are moderate enough to allow you to take action

2. Pay attention to the CABs that allow you to be productive in this situation

3. Extrapolate this success to other situations with similar challenges, but where the stakes are higher

THRIVING IN AMBIGUITY

A clear path in the Social Age is a rare thing. When it does appear, the clear path is often short and runs quickly into the fog of ambiguity. Leading has always been about taking risk and influencing others to take action when the results of those actions are not guaranteed. But at least you knew the odds that a given outcome would occur and how to influence those odds. The ambiguity that marks the Social Age is about a lack of certainty of the odds of an outcome occurring, or even the range of possible outcomes.

Ambiguity affects us all in two ways. First, it creates difficulty in choosing a course of action because our lack of predictive ability means we can no longer rely on the decision-making models we have used in the past. Second, the uncertainty associated with ambiguity creates a sense of unease and worry, especially when the range of possible outcomes is cloudy.[7]

Some of us naturally thrive in ambiguity. One such person we know is Angela Cretu, Group VP at Avon leading business in Eastern Europe. When we asked her about handling ambiguity she told us, "Once I have a stable point of reference, knowing who I am (strong identity, clear understanding of who we are as team or business, what we stand for, solid team around, etc.), I look at an ambiguous situation as a new playground with the anticipation and eagerness to get in, learn from it, and maximize the fun of playing with what I discover available."

Those who do find uncertainty exhilarating rather than worrisome and are comfortable moving toward a goal in successive approximations, reacting quickly to real-time events rather than sticking to a course of action. How can the rest of us become more tolerant of ambiguity?

There is no easy answer to this question. In fact, those of us who find ambiguity worrisome rather than exhilarating are likely to always find it so. Being a performative artist means being able to thrive in, rather than being rendered frozen by, uncertainty. You can do this by focusing on three things:

1. Maintaining your long-range goals but vastly shortening your action horizon. That is, keep your long-term goal in mind but plan for and take only an immediate action.

2. Reassessing and readjusting. After each immediate action, reexamine what you know and then take the next step. The trick here is not to become stuck in analysis paralysis. You will never have all the information you need, you just need to be able to recognize that your next step will not be a disaster—it can be wrong as long as it is correctable. It is this sequence of short-term actions, quick reactions, and maintaining the long-term goal that characterizes those who succeed within ambiguity.

3. Accepting and managing your anxiety. If you find uncertainty worrisome rather than exhilarating, you have lots of company. Whenever any of us feels anxious, we use CABs to reduce these feelings. Pay attention to the CABs you use. It is likely that they are all effective in managing your worry. The question is whether they are effective or ineffective in productively influencing those around you. Expand the former and reduce the latter.

IN SUMMARY

The social age is an age of constant ambiguity. The ambiguity we face forces us to lead within two paradoxes:

1. Having to hold values-drive points of view *while* acknowledging the validity of other points of view
2. Having faith in our ability to influence the events around us *while* accepting the tremendous levels of uncertainty

These paradoxes are driven by three realities of leading in the Social Age:

- That leaders will face multiple constituencies who expect a "share of voice" in setting direction
- That leaders no longer have the ability to control the flow of information due to easy access to mass communication tools and the widespread interconnectivity of constituents
- That less than certain understanding of both current influences and the probabilities of future events is part and parcel of leading in the Social Age

The Tenet of Social Leadership that helps a leader to address these challenges is what we call Proactivity—remaining active and having faith in your ability to influence the events around you. The productive CABs that drive Proactivity fall into three areas:

- Being a *Performative Artist:* the ability to remain credible to yourself and others when acting within a contradiction
- *Self-Belief:* a personal, fact-based belief in your capacity to succeed in a given situation
- *Tolerating Ambiguity*: the adoption of productive CABs to manage the discomfort and stress of ambiguity including shortening your action horizon, frequent readjusting of your path forward, and being accepting of a state in which you are not able to have full knowledge before acting

8

Connected Constituencies: Relating to Others Authentically

. . . you have to play a long time to be able to play like yourself.
MILES DAVIS

SELLING THE PLAN

After five months of work, the bulk package RFID label plan was finally ready. The team had sent the plan to Bob Roberts, IKU's EVP of strategy. As the management committee sponsor, Bob would need to approve the plan and then sell it to the management committee, the board, and ultimately the entire company. The team decided that Tom and Mary would take the meeting with Bob because schedules were tight and otherwise it would be weeks before all five of them could get together.

Bob got right to the point: "There is a lot of good work here and I see what you want to do, but I have some real concerns and I am not sure this plan is on the right track. I have seen a ton of stuff on this from everyone involved and have been chatting back and forth with some of the people in the trenches. After reading the plan, I am not sure if you are setting us up to move completely out of our core business in five years or if you are setting this new division up to be shelved in five years."

"Both," replied Mary. "We think the future of the business is going to move more and more toward gathering consumer insights, and RFID is just a stop along the way." They spent the next hour reviewing the details of the plan. Then Bob said, "I understand the details, I am just not sure I have faith in the solution."

Tom said, "Let me take you through this again and answer any questions you have." Tom started walking Bob through sales projections for potential new business and the investment costs for the new division. Bob was growing visibly more annoyed and said, "I told you, Tom, I get it. I am just not convinced."

Mary jumped in, "Look, Bob, everyone we talk to has shown some level of excitement about this. I know it means some staff dislocation and pain during the transition. Is this what is concerning you?"

"We have always been a growth company. Even when we hit some tough times ten years ago, we didn't lay anyone off. This will mean transitioning staff to these new businesses. Is that who we are? Will we be losing our identity, our brand?" asked Bob.

"I understand," replied Mary. "I don't have your long history here but I feel connected to who we are too. However, at our core I think we have always been about innovation. We are suggesting that we expand the way we think about the areas in which we innovate. There is going to be some pain, but over time there will be pride too. And success."

"Why not meet with some of the teams on the ground?" suggested Tom. "Let's go and visit the major teams gearing up to work on this. I promise you the energy is infectious. They would love to take you through what they are thinking in person."

Bob thought for a moment, his face softening a bit. "I would like to meet some of these people, talk to them, and hear some of this for myself. And," Bob said, turning to Mary, "if we really can position this as a strategy that extends innovation as our core strength rather than just moving slowly out of one business and into another, this may be a more acceptable plan."

Tom and Mary have a problem. Bob, the person most critical to their team's plan, gets it, understands it, and doesn't buy it. Tom's appeals to reason and logic not only fail, they threaten to make matters worse. Bob seemed to have gotten all the information he needed to form an opinion even before they sent him the plan. How do they solve this problem?

In the Social Age, information flows freely and quickly. This means that those you need to influence may believe they know enough to make up their minds before you even begin. The need to influence people over whom you do not have direct authority, when information flow is uncontrollable and points of view can be formed early, requires you to generate what we call Social Energy. This chapter is about doing just that.

In the early 1990s one of the authors of this book worked at a financial services firm with local retail brokerage offices across the United States. At the time, we had a common saying: "The three fastest forms of communication are telephone, television, and tell-a-branch." We had e-mail and phones but the Internet hadn't made an appearance yet. Even then, within our community of 260 branches and seven thousand people, events, gossip, and ideas spread like wildfire. Someone once fell through a plate glass window at a branch Christmas party in New York City, and everyone in Chicago knew about it within a day. When we created a new approach for cross-selling in San Diego, the offices in Houston were asking for training on it within days.

The spread of information across a community has existed for a long time. This was always a leadership challenge for sure, but it is not the leadership challenge of the Social Age. Today's deeply connected communities create the challenge of *social information*. Two things drive social information: "going viral" and our newfound willingness to "live life out loud."

According to Wikipedia, "Viral phenomena are objects or patterns able to replicate themselves or convert other objects into copies of themselves when these objects are exposed to them. This has become a common way to describe how thoughts, information, and trends move into and through a human population."[1] The spread of a story through the grapevine has been replaced with the immediate transmission of an idea, story, or piece of data directly and in its original form to everyone within a network and then to those that people in the original network are connected to. Sharing, retweeting, reposting, and so on have put the power of propagation in everyone's hands.

Mass communication was once controlled by those with an interest in curating content for the benefit of the organization or group. Within companies, leaders and communications specialists selected content for mass distribution based on company goals and with the aim of aligning viewpoints. The grapevine was always there, but so was management, which interceded to add the "company line." Today, mass communication is in the hands of everyone and information is transmitted by all who have an interest in sharing the information. This is a big part of the problem confronting our heroes in the IKU case study. Tom and Mary are trying to discuss the team's plan with Bob, but Bob has sought out information and had discussions about the plan with lots of people before Tom and Mary even got to his office.

Further, individuals no longer act as either passive receivers of information or transition points, passing the word along to others. In the Social Age we are encouraged to live life out loud, sharing our views with anyone who will listen. We can "like," comment on, and blog about everything that comes our way. Points of view are created on a community basis, with multi-way dialogue occurring with anyone who wishes to weigh in.

All this creates new challenges. Leaders once focused on speed, to stay ahead of the story, and on "sense making" or putting out a point of view to control implications and create alignment. In the Social Age, real-time communication and commentary make staying ahead of the story and controlling its meaning and implications impossible. The challenge today for a leader is not to "align" everyone to a single point of view but to generate and harness Social Energy to focus on achieving common goals.

One of the key factors in the complexity of the Social Age is that leaders must influence diverse constituencies who are simultaneously trying to influence one another. However, because leaders may have no direct authority over many constituencies, the traditional channels of influence—such as reward, punishment, and the chain of command—are rendered largely ineffective. The need to open up other channels of influence therefore becomes paramount. These alternate channels create emotional engagement, make social inclusivity happen, and, most important of all, help others discover meaning and purpose. They generate what we have been calling Social Energy.

BEYOND THE RATIONAL ARGUMENT

According to Mark Twain, "Get your facts first, and then you can distort them as much as you please." Twain made the clear observation that once someone or some group is fixed on a point of view, rational argument makes little impact. Once a point of view is strongly held, facts are simply interpreted to support the existing belief. No tool has been invented to serve this advice better than social media. Unfortunately for Twain, he lived a century too early to learn why this is so. As we now know, we do not see facts—we see facts through our own filters.

In 2004, researchers from Emory University conducted a study in which volunteers with self-described strongly held political beliefs were placed in MRI machines.[2] While their brains were being actively scanned, they were shown two film clips. The first showed prominent politicians that the subjects endorsed, speaking in favor of a belief the subjects shared. The second showed the same politicians arguing against this same belief. Everything in the film clips was completely factual and subjects were from both sides of the political aisle.

The results of the research were astonishing, and they confirmed something we've known for years: human beings do not regard facts as important when those facts challenge strongly held beliefs. The subjects ignored rational information that was factually correct and continued to make up their minds based on their beliefs and biases. Using functional neuroimaging (fMRI), the researchers were able to zero in on how the participants' brains were reacting to the facts with which they were being presented. "We did not see any increased activation of the parts of the brain normally engaged during reasoning," said Drew Westen, the lead researcher. "What we saw instead was a network of emotion circuits lighting up, including circuits hypothesized to be involved in regulating emotion..."

Notably absent were increases in activity in the area of the brain that is specifically charged with reasoning! What happened instead were spikes of activity in the "emotional circuits." Further, once the participants had found ways to either ignore or discount the information that conflicted with their beliefs, the circuits that mediate negative emotions got switched off and there was a blast of activation in circuits associated with the reward mechanism in the brain.

"Everything we know about cognition suggests that, when faced with a contradiction, we use the rational regions of our brain to think about it, but that was not the case here," said Westen. "None of the circuits involved in conscious reasoning were particularly engaged. Essentially, it appears as if participants twirl the cognitive kaleidoscope until they get the conclusions they want, and then they get massively reinforced for it, with the elimination of negative emotional states and activation of positive ones." What the study makes very clear is that once beliefs set in, it is very difficult to change them using rational information and facts. In our IKU case study, Tom learns this directly. The more he reviews the facts and the logical arguments with Bob, the more annoyed and frustrated Bob becomes.

This has significant implications for the Social Leader who is constantly in the position of needing to influence multiple constituencies, many with strongly held beliefs and some who hold views that are different from those of the leader. What are the options for a leader when he can no longer rely upon authority? And what are the options when rational argument becomes counterproductive? The solution is to generate Social Energy through emotional engagement, social inclusion, and purpose.

GENERATING SOCIAL ENERGY: CREATING THE UPWARD SPIRAL

Social Energy is created and sustained through the reciprocal and causal link between what we think, how we feel, and our physical state. These three factors all interact with one another to reinforce our beliefs,[3] creating a dynamic spiral that can be positive or negative.

Downward spirals narrow our attention as our brains react to perceived physical danger, thereby focusing all energies on the potential threat; upward spirals do exactly the opposite. Upward spirals lead people into broader "thought–action repertoires" and enhanced "behavioral flexibility." Whereas downward spirals lead to "excessive self-focus attention" and a move away from what matters most, upward spirals lead to "increased openness" and a move toward what matters most. Downward spirals encourage groups to close ranks and be defensive while upward spirals encourage individuals and groups to be more affiliative and to seek more connections.

For example, if a person (or group) believes a course of action is failing, he may despair for the immediate future. Despair may be "accompanied by rumination and withdrawal behaviors coupled with a sense of fatigue." These three elements of despair begin interacting dynamically to produce further negative beliefs as the brain seeks consistency. This is the downward spiral. The person or group may then begin to put up barriers or close ranks and misconstrue others' attempts to help as taking advantage of or harming them. They might withdraw and begin to constrict the actions they are willing to take.

A different person or group, seeing the same failing strategy, may

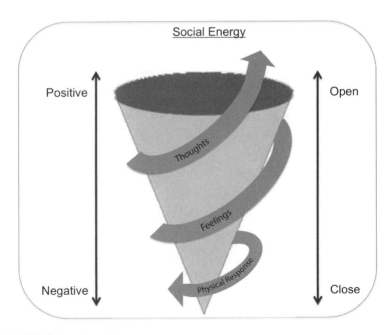

FIGURE 8-1 Social Energy

instead respond with confidence. Confidence may be accompanied by curiosity, outward-seeking behavior, and feelings of calm as well as physical energy. These three components reinforce one another, driving an upward spiral in which the group seeks new solutions and expands the types of activities they try to resolve the problem.

How can the Social Leader generate these upward spirals? The answer is to generate emotional engagement, social inclusion, and purpose. But how you go about this is crucial. The Social Leadership tenet of authenticity—relying on CABs that are consistent with your values and capabilities—is the linchpin to building the trust and credibility necessary to create the Social Energy of an upward spiral. Let's first look at the types of CABs that are needed in the repertoire of the Social Leader to generate an upward spiral and then examine what it means to use them in a way that conveys authenticity.

Let's look at how Mary from our IKU case study manages to create an upward spiral with Bob. Bob is annoyed and has already formed a negative view of the team's plan, repeatedly saying he "gets it but doesn't buy it." Rather than argue, Mary searches for the emotion driving his thinking. She helps Bob discuss how this plan threatens a core value of his and what he believes is a value of the company. Bob tells Mary that he believes this plan will create distance between himself and his colleagues on the one hand and with the employees on the other, and then he goes on to explain that he sees this as a threat to the overall purpose of the company. Bob is taking into account not only sales and financial projections but considerations around emotional engagement, social inclusion, and purpose.

THE FOUR BIG NEEDS

For human beings to operate at their best in any organization, they must have four needs met: the need for clarity and information; the need for emotional engagement; the need for social inclusivity; and the need for meaning and purpose.

Clarity

Take a look at the figure below:

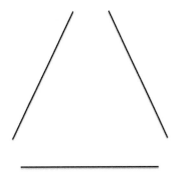

FIGURE 8-2   Gestalt Triangle

What is this? It is actually three lines. The odds are pretty good that you wanted to say "triangle." We all have a strong need to create clarity, to put the pieces together to create a picture. When we don't have all of the pieces we either seek them out or fill them in with what we expect to see. Before the Social Age, a leader played the role of key information source, filling in the missing pieces. This was a powerful tool in creating influence. By being the source of information a leader could shape the picture being created.

Today, an individual's network has joined the leader as a source of information. Consider the *Encyclopedia Britannica* being replaced by Wikipedia—the single authority was replaced by the community. We referred earlier to the 2013 Edelman Trust Barometer, which showed that social media sources are considered as trustworthy as corporate leaders when it comes to information about a company.[4] In the Social Age, this powerful tool for influence has been greatly diminished for individual leaders and shifted to the community. The implication is that CABs that centered on controlling the distribution of information have shifted from being productive to being unproductive. The Social Leader must look instead to CABs associated with the other three needs.

Emotional Engagement

Engagement is all about how much "heart" we have in our work. The difference between individuals and teams that "have heart" and those that don't are blatantly obvious. Key discoveries from neurology demonstrate that emotions are integral to the process of decision making, and not an appendage to reasoning, as the enduring myth of the "rational man" claims.[5] Connecting on an emotional level is essential to creating influence and Social Energy.

Ever since Daniel Goleman[6] and his colleagues published their foundational work in this area, a cottage industry has sprung up to teach emotional intelligence. Essentially, the advice amounts to "tuning in" to yourself and to others. That is, recognize the emotions you are feeling and acting upon, and recognize the emotions those around you are feeling and acting upon.

As we have seen, once individuals have "clarity" around a situation they will respond to new information emotionally. Information confirming the picture they already hold will be greeted with positive emotions, and contradictory information will evoke negative emotions and defensiveness. Helping yourself and others recognize these emotions and shifting them to a more positive footing will create openness to a wider range of ideas and even physiological changes such as increased energy.

Social Inclusion

The third big need is the need for social inclusion. The need to belong runs in our bloodstream and is part of our evolutionary heritage. Once again, new research in neurology shows that the mechanisms by which we are connected to others are biologically primed and "increasingly discernible in the basic structure of the brain."[7] In fact, social media is itself a demonstration of the human need to connect. The question is, how do you leverage that need effectively?

This is an area in which the tools and realities of the Social Age create opportunities that have never existed before. Groups and teams within traditional organizations are defined by structure. There are departments, and individuals are members of departments. There are project teams, and individuals are members of project teams. Both these structures are similar in a number of ways—they have a name, a purpose, and an expectation that members will share relevant information, meet regularly, and work toward a common goal.

The other thing they share is that they are exclusive; there are members and there are nonmembers, who are invited to participate only in special circumstances. The reason for this exclusivity traditionally was the cost and difficulty of meeting and sharing information and tasks. This barrier is largely absent in the Social Age. When you are trying to generate positive Social Energy in a community, the task is to make your movement go viral. As a Social Leader, seek out ways to extend the size of the team. Create as many opportunities for open forums as possible, where everyone with an interest can "drop in" to learn what is going on and contribute. Allow your project or effort to "live out loud" to the largest extent possible.

Purpose

The fourth need is the need for purpose. Here again, our brains seem to be hardwired to seek a higher purpose that helps us make sense of who we are and what we are doing. Purpose instills a sense of direction and motion, as it provides us with a larger perspective for why we are doing what we are doing. What can you do to tap in to the need for purpose and influence individuals and constituencies to work toward what you are seeking?

The answer is to find the "highest common denominator." It is important to recognize that everyone is motivated to act. It is just that they are not always motivated to take the actions you want them to take. Everyone acts for his own goals or for the goals of a group with which he identifies. If you wish to move an individual or constituent group to action, especially if you want them to act in concert with other individuals or groups, you must identify a *superordinate goal*. A superordinate goal is a purpose or outcome that lies beyond the immediate striving of the group and is one that all of the constituents you are trying to move have in common.

Shifting attention to this highest common denominator will help you reduce conflict and generate an upward Social Energy cycle. For example, at Interpublic Group, a major global marketing services firm where one of the authors worked, it was common for multiple agencies to work for a common client. It was also common for the overall client leader to struggle to generate influence across these different constituencies, as each had the conflicting goals of maximizing revenue for their own agency. The solution was to shift the focus to client retention, which meant creating advertising solutions that maximized impact for the client. This strategy of focusing on the highest common denominator was the key lever for global client leaders who had little or no direct authority over the vast majority of staff in different agencies serving a client.

GENERATING AN UPWARD SPIRAL OF SOCIAL ENERGY IN A NUTSHELL

The title of this chapter and this Tenet of Social Leadership is "Relating to Others Authentically," and yet we have barely mentioned authenticity to this point. Don't worry, it's on its way. So far, we have focused on the "relating to others" part of the tenet. The Social Age brings with it the reality of deeply connected constituencies, leading to information going viral and people living their lives "out loud," expecting to share points of view and information with the broadest possible audience.

This leads to an appreciation that information flow is no longer controllable and that individuals seek to generate a complete picture from many sources, not just you, their leader. The ability of a leader to control the flow of information, and with it the ability to directly shape others' understanding of a situation, is more limited today than ever before. Therefore, we have suggested that creating influence across constituencies is really about generating an upward spiral of Social Energy. Generating this Social Energy requires you to focus your CABs on three big needs: emotional engagement, social inclusion, and purpose.

Need	CABs Focused On
Emotional engagement	Tuning into your emotions and the emotions of others, taking this into account in communication
Social inclusion	Going viral—allowing as many as possible to "drop in" to learn about information, progress, and activities of any project you are leading that fits with their interest and passions
Purpose	Locating the "highest common denominator"; looking for superordinate goals that various constituencies can support together

In our case study of IKU, how do Tom and Mary generate the Social Energy to move Bob to a positive stance on their plan? First, they tune in to the values that Bob was defending and help him replace this with another cherished value—refocusing from loyalty to creativity. Second, they help replace the isolation caused by the idea of dislocating staff with inclusion, offering to bring him into the teams at work and experience their excitement. Third, they show him a higher level of purpose by linking the plan to the superordinate goal of innovation.

THE DEMAND FOR AUTHENTICITY

The subject of authenticity has long been important in philosophy and in popular discourse, and is now a rapidly growing area of interest for researchers in psychology. "To thine own self be true" is one of Shakespeare's most popular lines, and we all understand the value of authenticity and the qualities of one who is faithful to his or her "true self," whatever that may mean. But how do we judge authenticity and how do we learn to become more authentic? As the Miles Davis quote that opens the chapter indicates, "playing like yourself" doesn't come easy.

We think of authenticity in terms of a concept called the Personal Narrative. The Personal Narrative is the intersection of the stories we tell about ourselves and the stories others tell about us. The larger the

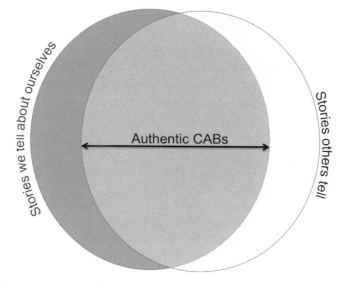

FIGURE 8-3 Authentic CABs

overlap between these two, the more authentically we are leading. Consequently, the smaller the overlap, the less our CABs authentically reflect who we are.

STORIES OF YOURSELF

The stories we tell about ourselves are derived from two sources. The first is intrinsic, who we really are: our values, our passions, and what we perceive to be our purpose in life. The second source is extrinsic, our sense of what others think of us. As Johann Wolfgang von Goethe, the famed German thinker, stated, "I am not what I think I am; I am not what you think I am; I am what I think you think I am."

If we derive our stories of ourselves largely extrinsically, we become what Erich Fromm called "a marketing personality,"[8] always striving to match who we are to what we think our audience wants. In this way, the shape and size of the circle that represents your story of yourself constantly shifts and changes, making it difficult for others to believe they know the "real you." This will make it difficult for others to view you as authentic.

How can you shift to a more intrinsic basis for your own stories, one defined by your values, passions, and purpose? The path to creating an intrinsically driven sense of yourself requires finding ways to address your own needs for emotional engagement, social inclusion, and purpose, rather than holding onto the ways you met those needs in the past. Dependency and a need for control cause us to "hold on" rather than seek. It is easy to feel dependent on the people and their reactions to our CABs that have helped us meet these needs in the past. When this happens we seek to control circumstances around us to avoid rocking the boat.

Of course, staying in tune with the values and interests of the constituents you wish to influence is crucial. However, remaining authentic means letting go of these past ways of meeting your needs and finding the confidence to seek new ways. By doing this, you will find you rely most on those CABs that are consistent with your values rather than shifting to please the crowd. Being authentic does not mean constantly using the same CABs, it means using CABs that are related to a consistent set of values.

OTHERS' STORIES OF YOU

Have you ever received feedback that seemed totally out of sync with your intentions? What you intended to convey was entirely different from what others perceived. One of us once bought his wife a frying pan as a birthday gift. She is an avid cook, and the intention was to support her cherished hobby (I swear). Her perception of that action did not match the intention at all, and that gap proved costly in many, many ways.

Clearly, something happens in the way we project our CABs that confuses, or in some cases fundamentally alters, the message we intend. Author William Randall refers to the story others tell about us as a *biography*, in contrast with the story we tell, which is an *autobiography*.[9] According to Randall, these biographies are not just static snapshots that capture who we are in the present moment. They are dynamic guesses about where we have come from and where we are going. So the stories others tell about you are not just based on some conversation or action or behavior you have displayed; rather, they provide a perspective on the larger purpose that others believe guides you and the values that drive your CABs. The challenge for the Social Leader is to shape the perceptions of others through communicating the deeper levels that drive and sustain who he is. The Social Leader must display and make explicit the passion and purpose that define him in order to bring together the internal and external portions of the Personal Narrative.

AUTHENTICITY IN RELATIONSHIP

Physicist Ben G. Yacobi provides a clue to authenticity's meaning when he describes it as a process of becoming rather than a static definition of who we are.[10] In that sense, authenticity is a "continuous process and not an event." Building on that, we say that *authenticity is a process of becoming who we can truly be, in relationship with others and in the context of the situation.*

Bill George, former CEO at Medtronic Inc. and now a professor at Harvard, has this to say about his research findings on authentic leaders: "...these leaders did not identify any characteristics, traits, or styles that led to their success.[11] Rather, they believed their leadership emerged from their life stories. By constantly testing themselves through real-world experiences, and by reframing their life stories to understand who they are, they unleashed their passions and discovered the purpose of their leadership." Jonathan Donner, VP at Unilever, echoed this idea in speaking about the future of developing leaders: "Authenticity, values, purpose are themes that are important to development as never before—versus competencies and capabilities. Character has become increasingly important versus a limited view of competence."

The Social Leader needs to create a story out of purpose and passion that others can relate to and find inspiring. When dealing with constituencies that are not within direct lines of control, the old parameters of loyalty have to be replaced by new parameters of trust. Authenticity can only be generated when you reach deep into the core of your life and find the purpose and passion that define who you seek to become.

IN SUMMARY

People listen with emotion. Emotion colors how they interpret facts and generates the energy to drive the actions they take. Capturing attention, focusing direction, and harnessing the Social Energy of diverse and connected constituencies is the true work of the Social Leader.

The power to harness Social Energy derives from addressing four critical needs in others: clarity, emotional engagement, social inclusion, and meaning. Focusing on conversations, actions and behaviors (CABs) that address these needs creates an energy that feeds on itself. Do so productively by speaking to the heart as well as the head and you will create an upward spiral of success. Do so negatively by ignoring the filters others use to interpret their world and you will create a downward spiral leading to cynicism and inertia.

The challenge of creating Social Energy in the Social Age is that the diverse groups we need to influence are connected to each other and communicate in real time, in multi-way conversations. Dealing with such a cacophony at the level of emotion and personal self-interest requires that a leader truly remain authentic to their own values. As Angela Cretu said, "you need a point of reference, a true understanding of who you are..."

Tending to others' perception of you as authentic means being aware of and addressing the gaps between your "biography and autobiography." The challenge for you, the Social Leader, is to close the gap between what you say about yourself and what others say about you. Your Personal Narrative, the intersection of what you say about yourself and what others say about you, is critical to remaining authentic.

9

Working with Social Information: Remaining Open and Adjusting Your Perspective

We cannot solve problems by using the same kind of thinking we used when we created them.

ALBERT EINSTEIN

LISA AND GENE MEET WITH HOSUR'S TOWN COUNCIL

It was a surprise to everyone when the bulk label RFID team's plan called for the new division to be placed in Hosur, a small town outside Bangalore, rather than in Hong Kong. But the need for IT resources outweighed the manufacturing cost savings in China. It was an even bigger surprise when Bangalore politicians seemed less than enthusiastic about welcoming the IKU expansion. Construction permits and other approvals were all being held up. IKU's legal department was making no headway in managing the infamous Indian bureaucracy. Lisa, IKU's purchasing VP, and Gene, VP of industrial design, got on a plane to India to meet with local officials.

"Look at this," said Gene. Before takeoff, Gene had downloaded some interesting information. The local paper had published an editorial saying that IKU's expansion was coming at the expense of people in three slums, who were being rushed into new, unfinished government housing. An environmental group had started a blog detailing how the IKU expansion would add to local industrial waste, and a local

IT professional group's website had more than two hundred comments on a thread about IKU importing staff from China rather than hiring locally.

Gene and Lisa arrived at the Bangalore town hall expecting to meet with the town council. Instead, they found themselves confronted with hundreds of angry people. It seems someone had posted the meeting on the Internet and it took no time for lots of passionate people to mobilize themselves. Rather than participating in a reasoned discussion, they found themselves listening to speeches from local politicians playing to the crowd.

Lisa leaned over to Gene and said, "This will all blow over. Let's just let this go on and then we can meet quietly with the town council and show them the proposal to provide some community support and donations. They'll agree and things will be fine."

"I'm not sure," Gene whispered back. "I am not even sure the town council is the only decision maker. Certainly it is not the only one influencing the conversation."

"What are you suggesting? We engage all of these people? I don't even know how to do that. I am not even sure they know what they want. Let's stick to the plan," Lisa said with conviction.

"Obviously, this is a mess," Gene replied. "No, I don't think we should engage at this minute. Let's talk to the town council members after this breaks up. I think we need to stay high level and not expect much. Then we need to figure out how to talk to these different groups to see what they really want and how we can help them or at least manage expectations. We are not going to walk out of here today with what we want."

Just then their conversation was interrupted by one of the speakers from the floor, who said, "The IKU people are here, what do they have to say?" Lisa grabbed the notes she intended for her talk with the town council members and started to stand. Gene put his hand on her shoulder, stopping her. He rose instead and said, "Hello, I am Gene Koss, we're here to listen."

Were Lisa and Gene ambushed? No. Were they caught unaware? Absolutely. Why? It's unlikely they could have predicted when they boarded the plane that the local council meeting they were headed for would turn into a multi-constituent free-for-all. However, they believed they were going to solve a straightforward issue, what we would call a "linear" problem. They had a construction plan and they needed permits; the town issued the permits, and the town council would want some positive community contributions to grease the wheels. Difficult negotiations were ahead of them, maybe, but it was a problem they could frame and address with a straightforward strategy.

What they found instead was not a linear problem but a complex one, a challenge with multiple independent influences creating an emergent situation that was largely unpredictable. Let's explore the nature of complex problems and then look at the Social Leadership tenet of openness, which is the mind-set necessary for addressing complex problems.

Most business processes and most approaches to leadership developed before the Social Age focused on reducing ambiguity and creating predictability and certainty. That was a critical and meaningful activity when businesses faced linear problems. Linear problems occur when the challenges facing a company are known and operate independently. For example, events such as the increasing cost of a critical product component or the appearance of a new competitor are independent events, and models can be built to predict the impact on sales of price changes and market share changes.

Complexity—one of the hallmarks of the Social Age—is the opposite of linearity; it occurs when multiple causes converge to produce effects that are unforecastable. The word itself comes from the Latin *complexus,* which means "entwined together." A complex system is composed of interconnected parts, and it exhibits properties that are not obvious from the individual parts. Complexity occurs when unforeseeable factors converge to create a situation that is not only unpredictable but also immune to the traditional rules of decision making because it is impossible to assign probabilities to different outcomes. As we noted previously, leading within complex systems tests our tolerance for ambiguity.

Complexity has three main characteristics: one, a complex system is self-organizing, which means it consists of agents whose actions cannot be controlled or predicted. Two, it is adaptive, which means that the diverse agents make independent decisions to interact with one another. And three, it is emergent in that the result will always be different from the sum of its parts. The outcome "emerges" as the situation evolves. In a nutshell, complexity is the absence of the data points and information that we traditionally rely upon to make decisions.

All of these elements were present in the situation in which Gene and Lisa found themselves. The town council, environmentalists, and local IT workers are all independent actors, and their concerns interact with one another to create additional complexity. Moreover, as these interactions occur, a spiral of downward Social Energy is generated, creating a movement away from the direction that Lisa and Gene are promoting. Further, as Gene pointed out on the plane ride, there were signals, disparate and dispersed though they were, that they were heading toward an unplanned, ambiguous situation.

In the past, the need for certainty has driven the way we behave in organizations, the way we make decisions, the way we communicate, and the way we develop our leaders. Although we have known for millennia that ambiguity is part and parcel of life and is an important ingredient in our creative impulses, our emphasis on measurability and predictability has rendered ambiguity undesirable. Curiously, an inability to tolerate ambiguity is returning in the Social Age as one of the main factors of business and leadership failure. Let's take a look at the impact that complex problems and dealing with ambiguity can have.

THE CURIOUS TALE OF NOKIA

Nokia was the world leader in the telecom industry in the early 2000s, and was among the most profitable companies in the world. With a ringtone that had reached iconic status, powerful brand positioning, and Keanu Reeves flipping open its phone in *The Matrix,* the company seemed destined for success. It also had an enviable track record of reinventing itself, transforming from a lumber business to a leader in the mobile phone business.

In 2013, Microsoft bought out an ailing Nokia mobile phone division that was unable to compete with Apple and Samsung. Nokia had a 34 percent market share in 2005 and as late as 2012, it still had an 18 percent market share. At the time Nokia sold its mobile phone division, it held a mere 3.2 percent share in smartphones. What went wrong?

What went wrong with Nokia is precisely what had led Nokia to its success: expertise in the cell phone manufacturing business. Over time, this became an orthodoxy—a fixed mind-set—that began shaping the decisions and judgment calls made by its leaders. Nokia's orthodoxy prevented its leaders from reacting to the radical disruption initiated by Apple and Google, which altered the core of the cell phone industry. iOS and Android operating systems transformed the cell phone from a phone to a crucial technological gadget at the heart of a community comprising stakeholders, such as app developers and prosumers, who are actively engaged in providing feedback and influencing the direction of smartphone development.

Nokia became increasingly isolated from consumers, who wanted to influence the user experience, not the hardware, and from developers, who wanted an easy platform to work with and a market to sell their apps. Despite having the patent for "touch"—the swipe function that all smartphones feature today—Nokia was hustled out of the smartphone market.

Nokia's problem began with a rather inconspicuous development in 2005, when Google acquired a little-known start-up company called Android. This was a classic weak signal. It happened in what Nokia saw as an adjacent industry, and thus was easy to ignore. Our interviews with several Nokia leaders, past and present, indicate that while the weak signal was picked up in some quarters, it was not seen as critical.

At the time of Android's acquisition, Nokia's mobile phone business was highly successful, and there was more than a fair amount of hubris in its internal culture. The dominant position of its Symbian operating system seemed unassailable. And in a linear world, where phones remained primarily voice communications devices, it was. But by 2010 the weak signal had become a major disruptive force. The success of Google's Android OS and Apple's iOS as platforms for apps vastly changed the nature of mobile phone use and led to a shift away from hardware manufacture—Nokia's home ground—toward user experience. The communities that grew up around the App Store and Google Play ecosystems changed everything.

Nokia's own operating system, Symbian, was falling short of what the developers in the newly emergent community wanted. They found it clunky and difficult to work with, and began focusing on Apple and Android. With the threat now clearly visible, Nokia reacted to the complexity by going back to what it knew best: manufacturing quality cell phones.

What Nokia leaders really needed to do was pay attention to the information that was coming in, first from the periphery and later from all over, and adjust their perspective. Agility rather than expertise was the need of the hour. Weighed down with hubris and the burden of past success, Nokia was not able to move quickly enough to abandon old positions and adapt to the changing world. It needed leaders to step back from the situation and ask fundamentally challenging questions that dealt with the social relevance of Nokia to the community of customers and developers. Instead, the questions stayed focused on functionality, technical improvements, and manufacturing.

ADJUSTING YOUR PERSPECTIVE

Nokia was the victim of a fast-moving disruption that appeared suddenly out of an adjacent space. This is something that happens every day in the Social Age: socially created information; the advent of global, networked communities; and the prosumers who participated and championed the evolution of the smartphone all created complexity—interwoven forces that defy predictability. Nokia's lack of agility and its inability to shift perspectives cost it dearly.

The ability to pick up information that may not be in your direct line of sight (part of your strategic direction) and to adjust your perspective quickly is crucial for leaders in the Social Age. Complex problems, by their very nature, challenge a leader's point of view and the strategy she is executing. In the case of Nokia, the more complex the challenge became, the more the leaders insisted on returning to strategy as the element to fix. Instead, a successful Social Leader accepts ambiguity and works to gather information and build new perspectives—new points of view—rather than make old ones fit. Let's look at an entirely different situation to uncover how Social Leaders go about taking in new information and adjusting their perspective.

LESSONS FROM A PRO

On January 15, 2009, at 3:24 p.m., US Airways 1549 took off from LaGuardia Airport for a routine flight to Charlotte, North Carolina. Ninety seconds later it was hit by a flock of geese. The pilot, Captain Chesley "Sully" Sullenberger, a veteran of forty-three years of flying, would later describe the sound of geese hitting the plane as louder than the worst thunderstorm he had heard growing up in Texas. With both engines down, the aircraft stopped climbing and lost all forward momentum. With a full tank of fuel and 150 passengers on board, the Airbus A320 was headed for disaster.

Captain Sullenberger's immediate reaction on taking control of the stricken aircraft was to radio air traffic control and announce that he was turning back to LaGuardia. This was an immediate, default reaction when dealing with a problem at this point in the flight, part of the established strategy. Of course, having the plane's engines shut down by geese was not a predictable event. The captain was cleared right away for the return to LaGuardia. Although managing the aircraft according to "the plan" in the midst of this unforeseen emergency could easily have occupied all his energies, Sullenberger continued to seek new information. He was willing to see information that contradicted his plan and quickly deduced that he might not make it back to the runway at LaGuardia. Seconds later he checked with the control tower to see if there was any other airport available in New Jersey and asked about Teterboro Airport.

He was cleared for that too, but he decided not to turn toward Teterboro either. Sullenberger began with the default strategy, realized this would not work, and announced *his* strategy—Teterboro. Under extreme stress, instead of trying to make *his* plan work when incoming information suggested it would not, he developed a third alternative.

Think back to a time when you stood up and announced a departure from the routine approach. It's likely you felt good about recognizing that the standard strategy would not work. As new information showed that your revised plan was not working, did you accept this and rethink it or did you recommit to your revised strategy, making minor adjustments to try to make this plan succeed?

Back to flight 1549...

After a protracted silence in the cockpit, which cabin attendants would later describe as resembling the quiet of a library, the captain calmly told the control tower that he was "going in the Hudson." For the second time in the three minutes in air, Sullenberger had challenged his own assumptions based on the information he was picking up, and had readjusted his perspective.

Sullenberger's decision to go into the Hudson was not a knee-jerk reaction to ditching the plane, but rather reveals his ability to function in a state of ambiguity. He chose that portion of the river for the landing because he had seen boats in the area that could assist in the rescue. At the time of takeoff, those boats were peripheral information, drawn from an adjacent area (the river), rather than his immediate focus (the airspace).

The lesson of this story is about not succumbing to the familiar and instead being able to operate in a state of ambiguity in the absence of known landmarks and cues. If one can do that, then ambiguity provides a medium for exploring alternatives that were earlier hidden by the lens of the familiar.

We see this contrast between the stories of Nokia and Sullenberger in the different reactions of and approaches that Gene and Lisa from IKU took at the town hall meeting. Lisa looked at the mess of competing viewpoints and constituencies in front of her and suggested that they forge ahead with the plan. Gene, by contrast, looked at the same situation and realized things had changed. The people they thought could make decisions and control the situation—the town council—were neither in control nor were they the sole decision makers. Gene realized that not only did they not have all the relevant information, they might not even have the right questions. He adjusted quickly and spun their approach by 180 degrees. Rather than viewing the meeting as a chance to make an offer and negotiate, he took it as an opportunity to listen and build relationships.

MAKING AMBIGUITY DESIRABLE

Being comfortable with ambiguity and even thriving in it is fast becoming an important leadership capacity in the Social Age. Those who flourish in ambiguity are able to suspend judgment, stay curious, and experiment with potential solutions rather than wait for the one answer. How can you develop not only a tolerance for ambiguity but also the capability to thrive in it? A recent series of studies by Michael S. Lane and Karin Klenke provides some clues.[1] Based on their research, Lane and Klenke suggest four keys to developing tolerance for ambiguity: mindfulness, creativity, aesthetic judgment, and spirituality.

We have discussed mindfulness already, and its role in handling ambiguity is clear. Ambiguous situations tend to push our brains to default to familiar patterns, and therefore a leader with low awareness is bound to use CABs based upon established patterns. What about the other three? What have creativity, aesthetic judgment, and spirituality to do with being better able to deal with ambiguity?

While there are many definitions of creativity, one that resonates was shared in a discussion with us by Ian Florance, a poet and organizational performance expert who is also an associate at the Psychometrics Centre at Cambridge University: [creativity is] "seeing connections between things, and making these connections frequently." That means being receptive to numerous and multiple inputs without squashing contrarian contributions with one's beliefs. Research suggests that the habit of finding "uncommon connections" can be greatly increased by spending time in the pursuit of hobbies and other avocations. This is where the concept of aesthetic judgment comes into play—having a number of different ways of looking at the world and perceiving beauty.

For a business leader whose time is spent in numbers, data, spreadsheets, PowerPoint decks, and endless strategic meetings, the need for a counterbalance that produces dissonance in the brain becomes very important. In fact, a piece of groundbreaking research by J. Rogers Hollingsworth studying 450 scientists identified the role that an "avocation" plays in the development of scientific discovery.[2] Interestingly, the avocations scientists in the study pursued bore no immediate resemblance to their scientific work; instead, the hobbies reported were all in the arts and the humanities. Like Einstein turning to music after he had spent much time pondering an equation, the arts "stimulate the senses of hearing, seeing, smelling—enhancing the capacity to know and feel things in a multi-model synthetic way."[3]

In the context of leadership, introducing spirituality may seem misplaced, but we are thinking about spirituality from the perspective of having purpose. We have already discussed the importance of purpose as a factor in generating Social Energy. In order to generate purpose in others, the Social Leader must feel a deep sense of purpose within himself. Career analyst and author Daniel Pink's definition of purpose is apt: "the yearning to do what we do in the service of something larger than ourselves."[4] That might take the form of finding a new way to delight a customer, solving a problem that has not yet been solved, or doing work for the joy and fun of it. Purpose is about why we do things, not how we do things.

So are we saying that business leaders need to develop artistic appreciation, focus on creativity, and have a sense of purpose? In a word, yes, but not because these three are valuable in and of themselves (which, of course, they are). The point is, to succeed as a Social Leader you will need to perceive situations from multiple and often contradictory perspectives. Aesthetic appreciation, creativity, and purpose push a leader's mind-set toward comfort with cognitive complexity.

COGNITIVE COMPLEXITY

Cognitive complexity is a psychological characteristic that describes a leader's skill at framing and perceiving situations in multiple ways. Leaders with high cognitive complexity process information differently because they use more constructs, categories, and dimensions to perceive relationships between bits of information. Leaders with high cognitive complexity use this capability to see relationships across many points and build relationships and influence people through networks.

What are the factors that influence cognitive complexity? Cognitive complexity is created when dissonant factors are brought together; think of a finance executive taking an art history class.[5] Cognitive complexity is a state we can develop by going beyond our natural tendency to seek uniformity and easy answers. In Hollingsworth's study of scientists, which we referred to in the previous section, he identified "internalizing multiple cultures" as a key factor that impacts a person's ability to be cognitively complex.

DEVELOPING YOUR COGNITIVE COMPLEXITY

Were the Nokia leaders not cognitively complex? It is impossible to make that assertion, as a business failure involves many factors. However, after discussing the topic with many Nokia leaders, we believe it would be correct to assert that a culture had come to prevail at Nokia where "object-centered" rather than "person-centered" processes and communication had become de facto. One Nokia manager who left the company in 2013 after the sell-off to Microsoft said, "We had become obsessed with a process-centered world in which there was a process for every process...we had stopped talking about why we existed, what drove us to be Nokia...it had turned into a machine." Hard words, and perhaps overdramatized, but the essence is apparent. Cognitively complex leaders tend to use more person-centered communication and are able to frame their messages in a way that helps others connect the messages to their own sense of purpose.

Cognitive Complexity	Linear Cognition
Open to multiple inputs and perspectives	Closed to new inputs and seeks quick answers
Willing to internalize scenarios that are not familiar and may disagree with beliefs	Making quick judgments on scenarios that clash with beliefs
Seeking out the unfamiliar with curiosity	Discomfort with the unfamiliar
Willing to "step back" and reflect upon and even challenge one's reactions to unfamiliar scenarios	Biased in favor of one's own beliefs, and preferring the familiar to the unfamiliar
Willing to have conversations with multiple sources of information	Inputs from a fairly predictable source – "old boys networks"
Ability to suspend judgment while taking in new information	Inability to listen to contrarian opinions and perspectives

FIGURE 9-1 Cognitive Complexity

Let's look at the factors that mark cognitive complexity in contrast with its opposite, which we term linear cognition.

One of the authors has spent a number of years teaching leadership programs that focus in part on building cognitive complexity. One such program, delivered through Duke Corporate Education, involves creating "immersion scenarios" in which senior leaders are pushed into the deep end of an uncomfortable experience. An example of this is an exercise called Dangerous Opportunities, which uses professional actors to push leaders into a place of discomfort and ambiguity.

Once, while working with a leading pharmaceutical company, we enacted a lawsuit involving an irate customer whose partner had died on the operating table, lawyers representing both sides, and the media. When company executives were immersed in this threatening environment, their default behaviors kicked in and their tendency to use linear cognition became apparent; they got stuck in the "how" rather than climbing up to "why." Our experience with these programs highlights some CABs that can help expand your cognitive complexity, and which you might consider for your own repertoire.

10 Tips for Building Cognitive Complexity

1. Become aware of your cognitive frames and challenge them
2. Expand the circle of your stimuli and inputs
3. Learn something new every day
4. Create projects pushing you out of the zone of the familiar
5. Expand your reading repertoire
6. Go back to your avocation
7. Travel and immerse yourself in new cultures
8. Seek out new eyes through which to see the world
9. Craft the story of your "why"
10. Become multidimensional in decision making

OPENNESS TO LEARNING: THE "GROWTH MIND-SET"

The tips in the list just presented are all about developing a growth mind-set. Think of the leaders you've known: how many of them were willing to challenge their own beliefs, take in new information, and adjust their perspectives? How many had rich avocations that they pursued with passion? How many of them consciously chose to immerse themselves in environments that were uncomfortable and challenged their beliefs? In all likelihood, not too many; the ones who did stand out from the crowd.

The reason not every leader engages in a growth mind-set is simple: as we become increasingly successful we come under pressure to use those CABs that made us successful. We start filtering out everything that seems extraneous to doing what we need to do to succeed. But the science of success is pointing out that, in order to succeed in complexity, we must be open to learning. Success in the Social Age is defined by the ability to challenge and overcome the limiting tendency we all have to repeat what has made us successful in the past. This means constantly looking to change the perspective from which we take in new information and enlarging the CABs on which we rely.

IN SUMMARY

The Social Age has moved us from a world of linear challenges—difficult but knowable and subject to defined probabilities for different outcomes—to a world of complex challenges that are unforeseeable and unforecastable. Complex challenges are recognizable from three characteristics: independent factors, the intertwining of the independent factors, and the emergent outcome that results from the intertwining. Over time, the sum total becomes greater than any of the original driving forces.

The danger when confronting complex challenges is reverting to the strategy with which you entered the situation. Revising and doubling down on an existing strategy is our most common response to an emergent complex situation and is frequently a nonproductive one. A Social Leader approaches new situations from a mind-set of openness. This is a learned practice, one that requires adding to or expanding the CABs in our repertoire to include those that allow us to cultivate creativity (recognizing a wide array of connections), aesthetic judgment (using a number of mental models to recognize patterns, and purpose), and purpose (connecting what we are trying to achieve to something larger than ourselves).

10

Social Scalability: Communicating in a Transparent World

There is no unique picture of reality.
STEPHEN HAWKING

BOB ROBERTS SELLS THE PLAN

Bob Roberts looked around the conference table at his bulk label RFID team and smiled. At their last dinner, following a successful conversation gaining the CEO's approval of their strategy for the new division, there had been laughter all around. Today the mood was battle-weary satisfaction. In the afternoon, with the team in attendance, Bob pitched the plan to the full management committee.

The plan was approved, but it was a tough meeting and Bob did not understand why. Miguel Valente, the CEO, was in favor. Bob knew that the team members had each been having individual conversations with their bosses, all of whom were on the management committee, and Bob used the same five talking points and presentation with the management committee that he had used with Miguel. Yet the meeting got off track almost from the beginning.

As soon as the presentation began the general counsel raised some questions, which opened the door for everyone else's comments. Soon the group was talking among themselves rather than to Bob. At every pause in the presentation a conversation about strategy broke out but hardly related to the points Bob was making.

At the end of the three-hour meeting it was clear that Bob was the only champion of the plan in the room. He received the necessary approval to go forward and it was clear that Miguel would support him, but Bob would be on his own to sell the plan to the company and bring everyone along.

When Bob got to his office the next day he had five urgent messages, all saying essentially the same thing. Details of the plan for the new division had spread overnight. There were already 112 comments about the plan from all over Asia and Europe on the company's internal blog, on a thread started the previous night in Hong Kong. Bob knew of a few unauthorized Facebook and Glassdoor pages IKU employees contributed to anonymously, and these were already buzzing with comments. Two trade publication websites had already posted small articles that attracted comments from people all around the industry.

Just as Bob was sorting through these there was a knock on the door. Nancy Dee, the head of HR, and Bob's communications VP, Casey Bridges, hurried in to ask about the plan to "officially" announce the new division and the changes that would occur.

"Don't worry," Bob said. "First, all of this noise is running about 50 percent favorable anyway. Second, I have already given this some thought and I wrote this last night. Here." Bob handed them a draft memo for distribution across the company essentially summarizing the talking points he had used first with the CEO and then with the management committee. "Casey, clean up the language if you need to, then you and Nancy get this out to everyone in the company today. That should calm things down."

"What about after that?" asked Nancy.

Bob looked a little annoyed by the question. He was surprised that he needed to respond to all of this "noise," as he called it, rather than simply announcing the plan in an orderly, structured way, as he had hoped. It was also clear that Nancy and Casey were looking for a response beyond what Bob felt was needed.

Bob replied, "Obviously, there is a detailed plan that spans a period of months to get the new division off the ground. As things become live we'll figure out a way to let the relevant people know what they need to know. You two should be part of that working team going forward, but for now this memo should suffice to let everyone know what is going on."

It was clear that the discussion was over, so Nancy and Casey did as instructed. Ten days later they were back in Bob's office…and things were much worse.

Did Bob truly understand what was going on? Was a memo the best way to counter viral news? Can the same talking points serve for such different constituencies? Clearly, Bob is out of his depth in the Social Age. The act of drafting a memo and handing it to the HR and communications people to "clean it up" so that it can go out to "everyone in the company" reveals Bob's mind-set and his approach to a Social Age challenge. He is clearly stuck in a time where communicating to the organization involved the following steps:

1. Decide what others need to hear.
2. Decide the facts that need to be given out.
3. Decide how the news should best be propagated.
4. Give a draft to the experts to make sure the language is right and there are no potential legal troubles.
5. Cascade the information all the way down.

Sound familiar? We've all been through this many times in our organizations: the endless meetings to decide what needs to be said, the drafts and redrafts to make sure the language is just right, with lots of obscure words to both tell and not-tell at the same time. Then there's watching the look on the Bob-like leader's face, as the committee working on the drafts gives him the final version and wonders if it's going to fly.

At its extreme, this process is called *spin*—it is based on the notion that possessing information is tantamount to having power, and therefore giving information away is giving power away. For ages, there has been a diffuse fear that the masses gaining access to information would lead to anarchy. Bob's fear is no different. Of course, that is not the way he consciously thinks, but his CABs are clearly influenced by some powerful scripts that he executes thoughtlessly. A common line heard at many top management meetings when discussing a communication strategy is, "Do they really need to know all this?"

There is an increasing polarization taking place between two groups in the world of organizations: Bob is part of one group, fearful of transparency and lacking the skills to communicate broadly to multiple constituents simultaneously. This group sees the dialogue of the Social Age as dangerous. The other group has either grown up knowing nothing but transparency or has adapted to it. People in this group are aware of the potential excesses of social media but realize that everything has up- and downsides—as long as the ups outweigh the downs, all is well.

The gap between those who expect a high level of transparency and those who continue to try to control the dissemination of information is not just a generational divide. In past generational transitions, the new cohort brought fresh ideas and their own sensibility while the previous generation controlled dominant technologies and social structures. In the Social Age technologies and structures are being shaped by a wide range of constituencies, including the millennial generation, who bring with them a transparency mind-set.

These realities of the Social Age make this an opportunity for evolution not revolution. We are not suggesting you throw caution to the wind and make *everything* transparent. There will always be sensitive information that, if given out too freely, causes more damage than good. Instead, make this critical shift: manage crucial, sensitive information but don't conceal your agenda; expect multi-way rather than one-way communication; and, most important, recognize that everyone has a megaphone.

HOW METAPHORS SHAPE OUR CABS

We've said that Bob's CABs are out of touch with the Social Age. Why? To answer that, we draw on the work of George Lakoff, the linguist who suggested that how we think and feel are shaped by the dominant metaphors we have learned.[1] One common metaphor is "argument is war." Once we have internalized this metaphor, we get accustomed to such phrases as, "He shot down my point," "Her criticism is on target," "He won that argument." These phrases, in turn, validate the original metaphor "argument is war," making the metaphors self-fulfilling prophecies. So the metaphors we learn help us create our social reality and become a guide for action.

To use our terminology, our metaphors shape our CABs. That is, metaphors are part of our "source domain," which contains inter-locked memories from our personal experiences that link closely with our values and self-image. Our source domain pushes us to "thought-lessly" activate certain CABs as we interpret a given situation through the lens of these old metaphors. Those of us who have similar life experiences and share similar values employ similar metaphors to understand the world.

What Bob doesn't realize is that his source domain is not able to connect with all of the "target domains," the collective experiences and metaphors of the constituencies he is trying to influence. They employ different metaphors and even a different grammar. It is almost as though Bob wants to control the flow of information as though he were communicating through stained glass—letting only a predeter-mined shade of light through—while his constituents expect to be looking through clear glass. Let's do a short exercise analyzing some of Bob's ideas about communication:

- People should know what is useful for them to know
- It is the leader's job to set the strategy and channel it to his people
- Too little knowledge is dangerous, but so is too much
- The leader decides, the troops execute: that's the secret of a suc-cessful company
- You have to be careful that your message doesn't get lost in the process
- Communication is important to get us all on the same page; we have to be aligned around one goal
- Social media is like washing and hanging out your dirty linen for anyone to see

Looking at these statements, it is evident that there is one core communication metaphor Bob carries with him: stained glass. The stained glass metaphor describes communication as an instrument for reaching particular objectives by coloring the way information is transmitted. It's all about control. One implication of the stained glass metaphor to which Bob unconsciously adheres is that there is the "controller" and "the controlled." The transmitter of the information (the leader) is the controller while the recipients are the controlled. In other words, the leader proceeds as if he is the only one who knows what to say, how to say it, and why it must be said.

The stained glass metaphor—very much a part of leading like a general—shapes Bob's CABs in the IKU story. The Bob character is not a rare one; we meet Bobs regularly in numerous organizations around the world. They are good, honest people who are trying to do what they think is best for their companies, not realizing that their source domain is out of sync with their constituencies' target domains.

Unless Bob and the rest of us begin leading like mayors and start building an understanding of our constituents' domains, we will fail to generate the Social Energy necessary to create influence. The problem Bob has is a complex one. He sees the world and the task of communication through the stained glass metaphor. Some of his constituents, likely those closest to him, share this metaphor, however, many of his other constituents do not. This means that they do not understand or trust the way he is communicating. This lack of trust immediately calls the message into question. And the metaphors that the more socially connected cohort carry in their domains—clear glass, crowd-sourced wisdom, living life out loud—cause them to respond to this misunderstanding quickly and publicly. How widespread is this disconnect in domains? Let's look at a few recent public examples.

THE END OF THE RECEIVED WORD

You've probably heard the infamous Domino's story repeated every time the topic of using (or even allowing) social media in your organization has come up in a meeting. In 2009 a couple of Domino's employees posted a revolting YouTube video of what they were up to in the kitchen.[2] The video went viral, and five years later the debate continues to rage about how to "manage" social media at work, with some companies invoking a "zero attachment" policy that forbids employees to post anything about their employer.

The real issue is a deeper one: as leaders, we have grown used to what we refer to as the "received word" syndrome, in which leaders propagate information and the rest just receive it. This notion of the organization's rank and file being passive receptors fits easily into the military paradigm. The logic stretches further: the notion of the received word rests on the assumption that there is only one story and it is one the generals know.

The Domino's employees who posted the video were not in the received word category, and clearly felt they were producers of information rather than receptors. Employees, of course, are not the only ones who can grab the megaphone.

When United Airlines broke a passenger's guitar and refused to compensate him, the irate passenger recorded a song about United and posted it on YouTube, where four million potential customers saw it.[3] The passenger didn't see himself as a recipient of the received word from United; he was a producer of social information, a prosumer. Take another example: after the British Petroleum oil spill story spawned the infamous line, "Well, it was only a small spill in a very large ocean," the Upright Citizens Brigade—a comedy theater and performers' training ground—produced a farcical video portraying BP executives around a table dealing with spilled coffee.[4] Almost thirteen million people saw the video online, and clips were shown on many news outlets. It's not likely that dealing with the Upright Citizens Brigade was part of any strategic communications plan at BP.

The question is, in an age of ubiquitous access to information and tools to produce it socially, can we prevent someone from speaking about a manager or a company? Today, every employee is potentially two clicks away from having his point of view go viral. But that's not all.

Glassdoor, an online site launched in 2008, has transformed the very notion of employee opinion surveys. On Glassdoor, employees rate their managers, the CEO, the workplace, the culture, and whatever else they choose to comment on; the information is available to anyone and everyone who has access to the Internet. The Associated Press referred to it as a "job and career site where employees anonymously dish on the pros and cons of their companies and bosses."[5]

Let's change the lens through which we are looking at social information. Social networks are a reality. Can we look at the opportunities here? The value of social networks has gone far beyond being marketing opportunities for companies; they have become rich spaces for collaboration and innovation that can engage entire communities. The techies call this phenomenon "social translucence," an evocative term for "digital systems that support coherent behavior by making participants and their activities visible to one another."[6] We love this term, especially as it is such an apt way of describing the technical side to generating Social Energy! Clearly, the metaphors that exist in the domains of those who live in the Social Age are not the same as those who came before. As we immigrate to this new world, we are well served to expand our domains and adopt new metaphors.

CHANGING COMMUNICATION

As a Social Leader, the way you must communicate to be effective with the various constituents you are expected to lead and influence is far more complex than ever before. Whenever you communicate with one person or a team of people, you are potentially talking to the entire community. When you communicate with the entire community, each person will see it as a communication just for her and expect to be able to respond and engage in the conversation. Transparency is the norm and everyone carries a megaphone.

The core principle of communication has not changed: communication is not so much about what you say but about what others hear. While that principle hasn't changed, the "others" were once easier to define. They represented a relatively fixed unit of communication: the person across from you, your immediate team, the larger organization, and so on. Now that "unit" has become porous. Your constituents are actively trying to influence one another on a very broad scale, and they have the means to do so. Information travels very quickly through social media, and in the blink of an eye what was said in one office can spark conversation around the world.

Our constituents' newfound willingness to "live life out loud" poses a direct challenge to communicating like a general. Fortunately, it also creates unprecedented opportunities for those willing to lead like mayors. We have to learn to change the lenses that were more in tune with the linear world. A mayor must learn and communicate through the metaphors that resonate with his varied constituents.

From Sound to Light

In the Social Age, the shift in communication is analogous to moving from sound waves to light waves. Sound is made of waves that travel through a medium, such as air. Light is both a wave and a particle; it can travel without a medium, even in a vacuum. Sound waves depend on the medium to produce sound. This, of course, is the underlying metaphor that led to Marshall McLuhan's famous dictum: "the medium is the message." Light waves travel independent of the medium. When they meet barriers, sound waves become disrupted and stop moving; light waves scatter and become refracted—changing colors—but continue and even expand.

In the linear world, the sound wave metaphor worked well. If a leader wanted to communicate to the organization, her team put a message together and the leader propagated that message to the organization under the following assumptions:

- Communication best happens top-down
- There need to be channels of communication (a medium)
- The recipients of the message are static and passive while the message is being propagated (recipients are part of the medium)

Gossip and water cooler conversations notwithstanding (seen as minor ripples to be managed), the production and dissemination of the message was controlled by the leader and directed through the organization.

Today, a leader's constituents are not passive receivers of information. Those in your community not only possess the same tools for producing and sharing information that you do, they feel empowered to share, comment, and add to the message. Constituents are no longer the medium through which the message passes; they are points of refraction, changing the color and scattering the message in unpredictable directions.

Moving away from the metaphor of the sound wave brings the cliché of "cascading information" into serious question. Here is a quick story that illustrates this change. One of us worked for a water company in Britain in the mid-nineties. The company was going through a massive transformation from a utility to a private company. One earnest manager who had bought into the consultant-speak of cascading information started off his meeting with the pronouncement, "I am here to cascade information to you that I received from the senior team last week, and at the end of this session, I want to see all of you cascading to the next level below."

Many in the audience had never heard the term *cascade* in this context. One of them dared to put up his hand and ask the inevitable question, to which he got this answer: "It's like a waterfall." The fact that the company maintained waterworks made that answer even more hilarious. In the cascade model, leaders let the water of communication cascade down to the less-fortunate masses who in turn cascaded to the ones below. The assumption was that, after all the cascading had been done, everyone in the organization would know the same message, and there'd be a lot of wet people.

The cascade model fits the linear age of top-down communication in which the executive level controlled the messages. The water company did something else that seemed natural to its executives but which is out of touch with the Social Age. Using the same cascade model, they had put together spreadsheets that detailed how much information was to be communicated at what stage, on a need-to-know basis. The drivers of the Social Age include transparency and socially created information in a continually flattening, highly connected community. The idea of compartmentalized information doled out as and when the leader sees fit is foreign in this world. Many of your constituents are digital natives who will not just see such information control as wrong, they will find it incomprehensible.

Communication as a Light Wave

Let's recall the properties of light. It is both a particle and a wave, it moves independent of the medium, even in a vacuum, and when it comes into contact with opposition it can scatter and change its color. Communication in the Social Age is like that. The medium is no longer the message. The message is the message and the media (multiple) are media. They interact in a complex way—independent, intertwined, and emergent—to create Social Energy.

What does this really mean? Let's start with media. Suppose you have something to say to a colleague. The medium can be one-to-one conversation. That colleague can then share that conversation (directly or indirectly) via e-mail, text, Twitter, social media, a blog post, etc., with the rest of the team, the rest of the organization, or the rest of the world. And every recipient has the same opportunity. The message spreads easily through a vast array of media.

Now let's take the content of the message, the particle. This particle is carried through the various media as the message propagates, but it changes substantially along the way. But it is no longer like the old game of telephone, where the message got slightly corrupted at each point of propagation. Rather, each reflection point—each constituent in the network who cares to—adds to, comments on, or even redirects the message, creating new meaning. In this new world, the Social Leader needs to focus on CABs that allow her to flex to different scales and types of constituents, no matter the original target of the communication.

IN SUMMARY: PRINCIPLES OF COMMUNICATION FOR THE SOCIAL AGE

What Bob referred to as noise in the IKU story was his attempt to put a frame around what had really happened: the story had gone viral because everyone had a megaphone. What does Bob need to do?

For Bob, and for those of us like him, there are certain key principles that outline what it means to communicate in the Social Age.

- Every individual who comes into contact with you is carrying a megaphone and has the tools to share his version of your message
- Everything that you communicate to an individual or to the members of the team has the potential of going viral
- Transparency, crowd-sourced wisdom, and living life out loud form key words in new metaphors within the domains of many of your constituencies. Communication is not one way and it's not two-way; it's a network that operates in real time

Together, these three principles suggest that the appropriate metaphor for communication is not control but rather the town hall. In a way, we are getting back to where we started this book: the communication metaphor of the town hall reflects the larger metaphor of the organization as a community. In a community, the controller and the controlled become obsolete divisions as control becomes self-organizing based upon principles of trust, authenticity, and collaboration.

By now these principles are familiar, and we have discussed in previous chapters approaches to developing or expanding CABs in each of these areas. When we think about these principles in the context of communication we see the underlying driver of successful communication CABs as agility. Agility here refers to the capability:

- To move across different scales of audiences in ways that build trust, collaboration, and authenticity
- To bring a community-wide conversation down to a meaningful dialogue with one person
- To be able to address the community-wide propagation of a conversation you have with one person

When you have a message you wish to convey, ask yourself the following questions:

1. Will the message I am sending make sense in whichever medium it is conveyed?
2. How will the constituents I care about most—even though they are not the "targets" of this message—receive this message?
3. What will the reaction be to the things I am not planning on saying when they become public (and they will become public)?
4. What would members of the constituencies I care most about say if they were in the room right now as we are discussing (or I am thinking about) how to convey my message?
5. How will I join the conversation once it gets started in the community to continue to influence and shape the message?
6. How open am I to other voices weighing in on what I have to say?
7. Once other voices weigh in, what will I do to refocus the message for my intended target?

If this sounds like you need to act like a politician whose conversations, actions, and behaviors will be covered and commented on by the media—well, that is the price of being a mayor. As a leader, you are no longer the general. You are the mayor.

Appendix

The following tables provide a list of indicators of productive and non-productive Conversations, Actions, and Behaviors in each of the five Tenets of Social Leaders. This list is not intended to be exhaustive but to provide guidance when reviewing the themes of a personal narrative.

Mindfulness	
Productive	Nonproductive
• I become quickly aware of my mind wandering and can refocus • I recognize when I am acting by rote • I can focus on what others are doing • I can wait as long as needed before making a judgment • I actively give attention to people at the periphery of the action • I have a wide range of interests • I can find a way to break through obstacles • I find a way for everyone to contribute • I clarify everyone's role and get everyone on plan • I act based on the particulars of the situation even if I am uncomfortable	• My mind easily starts wandering and sometimes I cannot recall where I started • I tend to go on autopilot easily • I end up focusing on others' intentions • I come to conclusions quickly • I tend to focus attention only on the people who matter most to the issue at hand • I enjoy developing primarily within my area of expertise • I wait to take action until conditions are most favorable • My philosophy is that if someone is not with us, then they are against us • I avoid directly telling others what to do • I act based on my past success, tending to rely on what I know will succeed

Appendix

Proactivity	
Productive	Nonproductive
• I am able to identify the values driving different courses of actions	• I take action because some things are "just the right thing to do"
• I respect diversity of opinion	• I champion causes that I believe in
• I work hard to view situations from others' perspectives	• I work hard to bring others to see the world from my perspective
• I have confidence that I can expand on my past success	• I have confidence that I can succeed in any situation
• I seek out novel situations with moderate risks	• I seek out situations that are either deeply familiar or highly risky
• I seek to understand why someone succeeded	
• I plan actions only for the short term while maintaining long range goals	• I accept success as a given; and focus mainly on examining my failures
• I constantly evaluate and readjust plans and actions	• I plan goals and actions over the long term
• I accept concern over uncertainty as a normal response, paying attention to the impact of the actions you take to alleviate anxiety	• I stay the course in the face of adversity
	• I fight to maintain a calm, confident posture in the face of uncertainty
• I accept contradictions as part of the bigger picture	• I try to resolve contradictions

Authenticity	
Productive	Non Productive
• I am aware of my core values	• I am aware of the needs of the moment
• I make my values clear to others	
• I monitor my conversations, actions, and behaviors for consistency with my values	• I tend to keep my values private
	• I act in accordance with the needs of the situation
• I pay attention to my emotional response to others	• I keep emotion away from my responses

• I tune into others' emotional reactions, respond accordingly	• I prefer to ignore others' emotions and focus on facts
• I open conversations up to anyone who cares	• I limit information to those who need to know
• I work to expand the scope of a discussion to include new and additional ideas	• I work to focus the scope of discussions to the core ideas
• I act from a sense of purpose	• I act from expediency
• I seek out common overarching goals to settle disagreements	• I recognize disagreements as opportunities to advance my agenda
• I seek out others whose passions, interests, and skills connect with my efforts	• I seek out those whose skills are instrumental in meeting my objectives regardless of their own interests

Openness	
Productive	Nonproductive
• I tend to seek out as many connections as I can among disparate concepts and actions	• I like to find the clearest linkages among a field of noise and distortion
• I spend time pursuing hobbies	• I focus my time on my core ambitions
• I seek out new learning and new information from a wide range of sources	• I direct my attention to the most fruitful sources of information
• I spend time and am curious about topics and subjects far afield from my area of expertise	• I prefer to spend time and attention in deepening my area of expertise
• I recognize the mental models I use to understand the world, and I try to find different ways of making sense of what is happening around me	• I have a single clear model of how the world works in order, which allows me to interpret and make sense of what is happening around me

Appendix

• I constantly challenge my core assumptions about how the world works	• I like to maintain my expectations of the way the world works despite setbacks
• I try to place my life and actions in a context larger than myself	• I like to be the center of my own universe
• I seek out projects that push me into unfamiliar territory	• I seek out projects that allow me to utilize and expand on my area of expertise
• I immerse myself in new cultures whenever the opportunity presents itself	• I like to learn about other cultures and then relate them to my own culture
• I understand "why" I strive, and why I seek to create change	• I understand what is the outcome or goal I want to attain

Social Scalability	
Productive	**Non–Productive**
• I pay attention to the effect of the medium in which my message is being conveyed	• Pay attention to the content of the message rather than the medium
• I am deeply interested in knowing the response to my message by both the intended and unintended targets	• I am deeply interested in knowing the response to my message by its intended target
• I expect others to weigh in and add their points of view to my message	• I expect others to carry my message forward
• I recognize that when I speak to one person I am also speaking to everyone at once	• I adjust my message depending on the size of the audience in front of me
• I provide all the information because I expect transparency to be the norm	• I make sure I tailor information to suit different audiences
• I expect private communications and discussions to become public	• I expect private communications and discussion to remain private

Appendix

• I am fine with a multi-way dialogue and recognize I may lose full control of my message	• I prefer to retain control of the message and amplify it to overcome the "noise"
• I learn the "metaphors" or filters through which groups with different backgrounds will "hear" my message	• I make my message as culturally unbiased as possible and stick to facts
• I am willing to expand and adjust my message based on multi-way dialogue	• I prefer to stick to my "talking points"
• I keep the purpose of my audience in mind when communicating	• I keep my goals in mind when communicating

Notes

Introduction

1. Zeke Miller, "Time Poll: Support for the Leaker—and His Prosecution," Time.com, June 13, 2013, *Time* magazine/ABT SRBI, June 10–11, 2013 Survey, Final Data, June 12, 2013, accessed November 18, 2013, http://swampland.time.com/2013/06/13/new-time-poll-support-for-the-leaker-and-his-prosecution/.
2. "What Are the Largest Social Networking Sites?," eBiz|MBA, accessed January 26, 2014, http://www.ebizmba.com/. eBizMBA Rank is a constantly updated average of each website's Alexa Global Traffic Rank and U.S. Traffic Rank using data from both Compete and Quantcast.
3. Jeanne C. Meister and Karie Willyerd, *The 2020 Workplace: How Innovative Companies Attract, Develop, and Keep Tomorrow's Employees Today* (New York: Harper Business, 2010).

Chapter 1

1. John Kotter, "What Leaders Really Do," *Harvard Business Review*, reprinted in December 2001, http://hbr.org/2001/12/what-leaders-really-do/ar/1
2. Actually, in 1990 ARPNET was decommissioned opening the door to commercial Internet service which was fully realized in 1995 with the decommissioning of NSFNET. All of this was driven at first by a U.S. agency called DARPA and later the U.S. National Science foundation.
3. "2013 Edelman Trust Barometer," Edelman, accessed March 8, 2014, http://www.edelman.com/insights/intellectual-property/trust-2013.
4. "ISC Domain Survey," Internet Systems Consortium, accessed April 12, 2014, http://www.isc.org/solutions/survey/history/.
5. Jaclyn Branch, "Social Media and Workplace Collaboration," SilkRoad, accessed February 20, 2014, http://blog.silkroad.com/index.php/2012/10/social-media-policy-workplace-collaboration-infographic/.

Notes

6. Steven Carroll, "80% of Employees Spend 56 Minutes of Working Day on Social Media," *Irish Times*, accessed December 15, 2013, http://www.irishtimes.com/news/80-of-employees-spend-56-minutes-of-working-day-on-social-media-1.1384090.

7. Edwin Paul Hollander, *Inclusive Leadership: The Essential Leader-Follower Relationship* (New York: Routledge, 2009).

8. Barbara Nussbaum, Sudhanshu Palsule, and Velaphi Mkhize, *Personal Growth, African Style* (London: Penguin Books, 2010).

Chapter 2

1. Dee Hock, *Birth of the Chaordic Age* (San Francisco: Berrett-Koehler Publishers, 2000).

2. "2013 CEO Study: Leading in Context," Duke Corporate Education, http://www.dukece.com/elements/docs/LeadingInContext.pdf

Chapter 3

1. John D. Ingalls, *Human Energy: The Critical Factor for Individuals and Organizations* (Austin, TX: Learning Concepts, 1979).

2. Carl Jung. "The Transcendent Function," in *The Portable Jung*, ed. Joseph Campbell (New York: Penguin Books, 1976).

3. Fred Kofman, *Conscious Business: How to Build Value through Values* (Boulder, CO: Sounds True, 2006).

4. Henry P. Sims and Dennis A. Gioia, *The Thinking Organization* (San Francisco: Jossey-Bass, 1986).

Chapter 4

1. Morgan W. McCall, Michael M. Lombardo, and Ann M. Morrison, *The Lessons of Experience: How Successful Executives Develop on the Job* (Lexington, MA: Lexington Books, 1988).

2. Joseph Campbell, *The Hero with a Thousand Faces*, 3rd ed. (Novato, CA: New World Library, 2008).

3. We strongly recommend reading either *The Hero with a Thousand Faces* by Joseph Campbell or *The Power of Myth* by Joseph Campbell and Bill Moyer to truly understand this powerful concept of "monomyth."

Chapter 5

1. Adapted from Ronald Heifetz and Donald Laurie, "The Work of Leadership," *Harvard Business Review*, January-February, 75 (1) (1997): 124–134;

and Ronald Heifetz and Martin Linsky, *Leadership on the Line: Staying Alive through the Dangers of Leading* (Boston: Harvard Business School Press, 2002).

2. Martin E. P. Seligman, *Authentic Happiness: Using the New Positive Psychology to Realize Your Potential for Lasting Fulfillment* (New York: Free Press, 2004).

3. Morgan W. McCall, Michael M. Lombardo, and Ann M. Morrison, *The Lessons of Experience: How Successful Executives Develop on the Job* (Lexington, MA: Lexington Books, 1988).

4. Campbell, *The Hero with a Thousand Faces.*

Chapter 6

1. Nicholas Nassim Taleb, *The Black Swan: The Impact of the Highly Improbable*, 2nd ed. (New York: Random House Trade Paperbacks, 2010).

2. Mike Canning and Eamonn Kelly, "Dynamism and Discontinuity: Eight Trends in the Business Environment that Will Shape Strategy," *The European Business Review.* September–October (2013): 26.

3. Will Mitchell, "Organization and Innovation: Organizational Strategies for Leading Discontinuous Change," The Fuqua School of Business, Duke University, September 2009. https://faculty.fuqua.duke.edu/~willm/bio/TeachingMaterials/0Readings/ChangeModeReadings/OrganizationalInnovation_LeadingChange.pdf

4. "The mindfulness business," *The Economist*, November 16, 2013, http://www.economist.com/news/business/21589841-western-capitalism-looking-inspiration-eastern-mysticism-mindfulness-business

5. Jeremy Hunter and Michael Chaskalson. "Making the Mindful Leader," in *The Wiley-Blackwell Handbook of the Psychology of Leadership, Change and Organizational Development*, ed. H. Skipton Leonard et al. (Hoboken, NJ: Wiley-Blackwell, 2013), 195–220.

6. Elina Hiltunen, "Was It a Wild Card or Just Our Blindness to Gradual Change?" *Journal of Future Studies* Vol. 11, No. 2 (2006): 61–74.

7. Hunter and Chaskalson, "Making the Mindful Leader."

8. Hunter and Chaskalson describe three separate studies (Guth et al, 1982; Bolton and Zwick, 1995; and Kirk et al, 2011) showing how individuals trained in temporal mindfulness performed better on the classic social psychology experiment known as the Ultimatum Game.

9. Bill George, "Mindfulness Helps You Become a Better Leader," *Harvard Business Review*, accessed April 26, 2014, http://blogs.hbr.org/2012/10/mindfulness-helps-you-become-a/.

Notes

10. Hunter and Chaskalson, "Making the Mindful Leader."
11. James S. Uleman and John A. Bargh, *Unintended Thought* (New York: Guilford Press, 1989).
12. Paul Schoemaker and George S. Day. "How to Make Sense of Weak Signals." *MIT Sloan Management Review* 50, No. 3 (2009): 81–89.
13. Nate Silver, *The Signal and the Noise: Why So Many Predictions Fail—but Some Don't* (New York: Penguin Press, 2012), 38.
14. Bernard M. Bass and Ruth Bass, *The Bass Handbook of Leadership: Theory, Research, and Managerial Applications*, 4th ed. (New York: Free Press, 2008).
15. H. A. Murray, *Explorations in Personality* (New York: Oxford University Press, 1938).
16. Brian R. Little, *Personal Project Pursuit: Goals, Action, and Human Flourishing* (Mahwah, NJ: Lawrence Erlbaum Associations, 2007).

Chapter 7

1. William Shakespeare, *Hamlet*, ed. Harold Jenkins (London: Methuen, 1982).
2. "2013 CEO Study: Leading in Context," 2.
3. "2013 CEO Study: Leading in Context," 15.
4. S. Gallagher, "Philosophical Conceptions of the Self: Implications for Cognitive Science," *Trends in Cognitive Sciences* 4 (2000): 14–21.
5. Jürgen Habermas, *The Philosophical Discourse of Modernity: Twelve Lectures* (Cambridge, MA: MIT Press, 1987), 46.
6. Albert Bandura. "On the Functional Properties of Perceived Self-Efficacy Revisited," *Journal of Management* Vol. 38, No. 1 (2012), 9–44.
7. Adrian Furnham and Joseph Marks, "Tolerance of Ambiguity: A Review of the Recent Literature," *Psychology* Vol. 4, No.9 (2013), 717–728.

Chapter 8

1. Wikipedia contributors, "Viral Phenomenon," *Wikipedia, The Free Encyclopedia*, accessed January 16, 2014, http://en.wikipedia.org/wiki/Viral_phenomenon.
2. Drew Westen et al, "Neural Bases of Motivated Reasoning: An fMRI Study of Emotional Constraints on Partisan Political Judgment in the 2004 U.S. Presidential Election," *Journal of Cognitive Neuroscience* Vol. 18, No. 11 (2006): 1947-1958.

Notes

3. Todd Kashdan, *Mindfulness, Acceptance, and Positive Psychology: The Seven Foundations of Well-Being* (Oakland, CA: Context Press, 2013).
4. "2013 Edelman Trust Barometer," accessed March 8, 2014, http://www.edelman.com/insights/intellectual-property/trust-2013.
5. Antonio Damasio, *Descartes' Error: Emotion, Reason, and the Human Brain* (New Jersey, NJ: Putnam Publishing Group, 1994).
6. Daniel Goleman, Richard E. Boyatzis, and Annie McKee. *Primal Leadership: Realizing the Power of Emotional Intelligence* (Boston, MA: Harvard Business School Press, 2002).
7. The Commission on Children at Risk, *Hardwired to Connect: The New Scientific Case for Authoritative Communities* (New York: Broadway Publications, 2003).
8. Fromm, Erich. *Escape from Freedom*. New York: H. Holt, 1994.
9. William Lowell Randall, *The Stories We Are: An Essay on Self-Creation* (Toronto: University of Toronto Press, 1995).
10. Ben G. Yacobi, "Philosophy Now," *The Limits of Authenticity* Vol. 92, September/October (2012): 28–30.
11. Bill George, "Mindfulness Helps You Become a Better Leader." *Harvard Business Review*, accessed April 26, 2014, http://blogs.hbr.org/2012/10/mindfulness-helps-you-become-a/.

Chapter 9

1. Michael S. Lane and Karin Klenke, "The Ambiguity Tolerance Interface: A Modified Social Cognitive Model for Leading Under Uncertainty," *Journal of Leadership & Organizational Studies* 10 (2004): 69–81.
2. J. Rogers Hollingsworth, "High Cognitive Complexity and the Making of Major Scientific Discoveries," in *Knowledge, Communication and Creativity*, eds. Arnaud Sales and Marcel Fournier (London: SAGE Publications, 2007), 129–155.
3. Hollingsworth, "High Cognitive Complexity and the Making of Major Scientific Discoveries."
4. Daniel H. Pink, *Drive: The Surprising Truth About What Motivates Us* (New York, NY: Riverhead Books, 2009).
5. Mihaly Csikszentmihalyi, *The Evolving Self: A Psychology for the Third Millennium* (New York: Harper Collins, 1993).

191

Notes

Chapter 10

1. George Lakoff and Mark Johnson, *Metaphors We Live By* (Chicago: University of Chicago Press, 1980).
2. Klaus Krippendorf, "Major Metaphors of Communication and Some Constructivist Reflections on Their Use," *Cybernetics & Human Knowing* Vol. 2, No. 1 (1993): 3–25.
3. Stephanie Clifford, "Video Prank at Domino's Taints Brand," *New York Times*, accessed April 15, 2014, http://www.nytimes.com/2009/04/16/business/media/16dominos.html?_r=0.
4. Mark Tran, "Singer gets his revenge on United Airlines and soars to fame," *The Guardian*, accessed May 2, 2014, http://www.theguardian.com/news/blog/2009/jul/23/youtube-united-breaks-guitars-video.
5. "BP Spills Coffee: a PARODY by UCB Comedy." YouTube. Accessed May 2, 2014. http://www.youtube.com/watch?v=2AAa0gd7ClM.
6. The Associated Press, "Employees rate their employers, CEOs on Glassdoor," *CBC News*, accessed May 2, 2014, http://www.cbc.ca/news/business/employees-rate-their-employers-ceos-on-glassdoor-1.1314945.
7. Thomas Erickson and Wendy A. Kellogg, "Social Translucence: An Approach to Support Designing Systems that Support Social Processes," *ACM Transactions on Computer-Human Interactions* Vol. 7, No. 1 (2000): 59–83.

References

Bandura, Albert. "On the Functional Properties of Perceived Self-Efficacy Revisited." *Journal of Management* Vol. 38, No. 1 (2012), 9–44.

Bass, Bernard M., and Ruth Bass. *The Bass Handbook of Leadership: Theory, Research, and Managerial Applications*, 4th edition. New York: Free Press, 2008.

Branch, Jaclyn. "Social Media and Workplace Collaboration." SilkRoad. Accessed February 20, 2014. http://blog.silkroad.com/index.php/2012/10/social-media-policy-workplace-collaboration-infographic/.

Campbell, Joseph. *The Hero with a Thousand Faces*, 3rd edition. Novato, CA: New World Library, 2008.

Caning, Mike and Eamonn Kelly. "Dynamism and Discontinuity: Eight Trends in the Business Environment that Will Shape Strategy." *The European Business Review.* September–October (2013): 26.

Carroll, Steven. "80% of Employees Spend 56 Minutes of Working Day on Social Media." *Irish Times.* Accessed December 15, 2013. http://www.irishtimes.com/news/80-of-employees-spend-56-minutes-of-working-day-on-social-media-1.1384090.

Clifford, Stephanie. "Video Prank at Domino's Taints Brand." *New York Times*, Accessed April 15, 2014. http://www.nytimes.com/2009/04/16/business/media/16dominos.html?_r=0.

Csikszentmihalyi, Mihaly. *The Evolving Self: A Psychology for the Third Millennium.* New York: Harper Collins, 1993.

Damasio, Antonio. *Descartes' Error: Emotion, Reason, and the Human Brain.* New Jersey, NJ: Putnam Publishing Group, 1994.

Duke Corporate Education. "2013 CEO Study: Leading in Context." http://www.dukece.com/elements/docs/LeadingInContext.pdf

Edelman. "2013 Edelman Trust Barometer." Accessed March 8, 2014. http://www.edelman.com/insights/intellectual-property/trust-2013.

Erickson, Thomas and Wendy A. Kellogg. "Social Translucence: An Approach to Support Designing Systems that Support Social Processes." *ACM Transactions on Computer-Human Interactions* Vol. 7, No. 1 (2000): 59–83.

References

Fromm, Erich. *Escape from Freedom*. New York: H. Holt, 1994.

Furnham, Adrian and Joseph Marks. "Tolerance of Ambiguity: A Review of the Recent Literature." *Psychology* Vol. 4, No.9 (2013), 717–728.

Gallagher, S. "Philosophical Conceptions of the Self: Implications for Cognitive Science." *Trends in Cognitive Sciences* 4 (2000): 14–21.

George, Bill, "Mindfulness Helps You Become a Better Leader." *Harvard Business Review*, accessed April 26, 2014, http://blogs.hbr.org/2012/10/mindfulness-helps-you-become-a/.

Goleman, Daniel, Richard E. Boyatzis, and Annie McKee. *Primal Leadership: Realizing the Power of Emotional Intelligence*. Boston, MA: Harvard Business School Press, 2002.

Habermas, Jürgen. *The Philosophical Discourse of Modernity: Twelve Lectures*. Cambridge, MA: MIT Press, 1987.

Heifetz, Ronald, and Donald Laurie. "The Work of Leadership," *Harvard Business Review*, January-February, 75 (1) (1997): 124–134;

Heifetz, R., and Martin Linsky. *Leadership on the Line: Staying Alive through the Dangers of Leading*. Boston: Harvard Business School Press, 2002.

Hiltunen, Elina. "Was It a Wild Card or Just Our Blindness to Gradual Change?" *Journal of Future Studies* Vol. 11, No. 2 (2006): 61–74.

Hock, Dee. *Birth of the Chaordic Age*. San Francisco: Berrett-Koehler Publishers, 2000.

Hollander, Edwin Paul. *Inclusive Leadership: The Essential Leader-Follower Relationship*. New York: Routledge, 2009.

Hollingsworth, J. Rogers. "High Cognitive Complexity and the Making of Major Scientific Discoveries." In *Knowledge, Communication and Creativity*, edited by Arnaud Sales and Marcel Fournier. London: SAGE Publications, 2007.

Hunter, Jeremy and Michael Chaskalson. "Making the Mindful Leader." In *The Wiley-Blackwell Handbook of the Psychology of Leadership, Change and Organizational Development*, edited by H. Skipton Leonard et al. Hoboken, NJ: Wiley-Blackwell, 2013.

Ingalls, John D. *Human Energy: The Critical Factor for Individuals and Organizations*. Austin, TX: Learning Concepts, 1979.

Internet Systems Consortium. "ISC Domain Survey." Accessed April 12, 2014. http://www.isc.org/solutions/survey/history/.

Jung, Carl. "The Transcendent Function." In *The Portable Jung*, edited by Joseph Campbell. New York: Penguin Books, 1976.

References

Kashdan, Todd. *Mindfulness, Acceptance, and Positive Psychology: The Seven Foundations of Well-Being.* Oakland, CA: Context Press, 2013.

Kofman, Fred. *Conscious Business: How to Build Value through Values.* Boulder, CO: Sounds True, 2006.

Kotter, John. "What Leaders Really Do," *Harvard Business Review*, reprinted in December 2001. http://hbr.org/2001/12/what-leaders-really-do/ar/1

Krippendorf, Klaus. "Major Metaphors of Communication and Some Constructivist Reflections on Their Use." *Cybernetics & Human Knowing* Vol. 2, No. 1 (1993): 3–25.

Lakoff, George and Mark Johnson. *Metaphors We Live By.* Chicago: University of Chicago Press, 1980.

Lane, Michael S., and Karin Klenke. "The Ambiguity Tolerance Interface: A Modified Social Cognitive Model for Leading Under Uncertainty." *Journal of Leadership & Organizational Studies* 10 (2004): 69–81.

Little, Brian R. *Personal Project Pursuit: Goals, Action, and Human Flourishing.* Mahwah, NJ: Lawrence Erlbaum Associations, 2007.

McCall, Morgan W., Michael M. Lombardo, and Ann M. Morrison. *The Lessons of Experience: How Successful Executives Develop on the Job.* Lexington, MA: Lexington Books, 1988.

Meister, Jeanne C., and Karie Willyerd. *The 2020 Workplace: How Innovative Companies Attract, Develop, and Keep Tomorrow's Employees Today.* New York: Harper Business, 2010.

Miller, Zeke. "Time Poll: Support for the Leaker—and His Prosecution." Time.com, June 13, 2013. *Time* magazine/ABT SRBI. Accessed November 18, 2013. http://swampland.time.com/2013/06/13/new-time-poll-support-for-the-leaker-and-his-prosecution/.

Mitchell, Will. "Organization and Innovation: Organizational Strategies for Leading Discontinuous Change." The Fuqua School of Business, Duke University, September 2009. https://faculty.fuqua.duke.edu/~willm/bio/TeachingMaterials/0Readings/ChangeModeReadings/OrganizationalInnovation_LeadingChange.pdf

Murray, H. A. *Explorations in Personality.* New York: Oxford University Press, 1938.

Nussbaum, Barbara, Sudhanshu Palsule, and Velaphi Mkhize, *Personal Growth, African Style.* London: Penguin Books, 2010.

Pink, Daniel H. *Drive: The Surprising Truth About What Motivates Us.* New York, NY: Riverhead Books, 2009.

References

Randall, William Lowell. *The Stories We Are: An Essay on Self-Creation*. Toronto: University of Toronto Press, 1995.

Schoemaker, Paul and George S. Day. "How to Make Sense of Weak Signals." *MIT Sloan Management Review* 50, No. 3 (2009): 81–89.

Seligman, Martin E. P. *Authentic Happiness: Using the New Positive Psychology to Realize Your Potential for Lasting Fulfillment*. New York: Free Press, 2004.

Shakespeare, William. *Hamlet*, edited by Harold Jenkins. London: Methuen, 1982.

Silver, Nate. *The Signal and the Noise: Why So Many Predictions Fail—but Some Don't*. New York: Penguin Press, 2012.

Sims, Henry P., and Dennis A. Gioia. *The Thinking Organization*. San Francisco: Jossey-Bass, 1986.

Taleb, Nicholas Nassim. *The Black Swan: The Impact of the Highly Improbable*, 2nd edition. New York: Random House Trade Paperbacks, 2010.

The Associated Press. "Employees rate their employers, CEOs on Glassdoor." *CBC News*. Accessed May 2, 2014. Http://www.cbc.ca/news/business/employees-rate-their-employers-ceos-on-glassdoor-1.1314945.

The Commission on Children at Risk. *Hardwired to Connect: The New Scientific Case for Authoritative Communities*. New York: Broadway Publications, 2003.

The Economist. "The mindfulness business." November 16, 2013. http://www.economist.com/news/business/21589841-western-capitalism-looking-inspiration-eastern-mysticism-mindfulness-business

Tran, Mark. "Singer gets his revenge on United Airlines and soars to fame." *The Guardian*. Accessed May 2, 2014. http://www.theguardian.com/news/blog/2009/jul/23/youtube-united-breaks-guitars-video.

Uleman, James S., and John A. Bargh. *Unintended Thought*. New York: Guilford Press, 1989.

Westen, Drew, Pavel S. Blagov, Keith Harenski, Clint Kilts, and Stephen Hamann. "Neural Bases of Motivated Reasoning: An fMRI Study of Emotional Constraints on Partisan Political Judgment in the 2004 U.S. Presidential Election." *Journal of Cognitive Neuroscience* Vol. 18, No. 11 (2006): 1947-1958.

Wikipedia contributors. "Viral Phenomenon." *Wikipedia, The Free Encyclopedia*. Accessed January 16, 2014. http://en.wikipedia.org/wiki/Viral_phenomenon.

Yacobi, Ben G. "Philosophy Now." *The Limits of Authenticity* Vol. 92, September/October (2012): 28–30.

YouTube. "BP Spills Coffee: a PARODY by UCB Comedy." Accessed May 2, 2014. http://www.youtube.com/watch?v=2AAa0gd7ClM

Index

Index

behavioral flexibility, 140

biography, 149

British Petroleum oil spill, 173

business organization as community
affinity principles, 31–34
architecture of, 30
connectivity principles, 32, 34
leader as mayor concept, 41
membership principles, 31, 33
traditional organization to business
community, 23–26
UBM company transition, 19–21,
26–30

C

CABs (conversations, actions, and
behaviors)
and mindfulness, 106–107
and Personal Narrative, 44, 50
and social leadership development,
72, 77

calmness, 142

Campbell, Joseph
The Hero with a Thousand Faces, 56

clarity, need for, 143

cognitive complexity
developing your, 163–164
factors influencing, 162–163
immersion scenarios, 164
internalizing multiple cultures as key
factor of, 163
and linear cognition, 163–164

communication
cascade model of, 176
collective experiences and metaphors,
170–172
gossip and water cooler conversation,
175
leadership challenges unique to
Social Age, 10
as light wave metaphor, 177

principles for the Social Age,
177–179
shift in, 174–178
sound wave metaphor, 175
top-down, 176

community-based organization
affinity principles, 31–34
architecture of, 30
connectivity principles, 32, 34
leader as mayor concept, 41
membership principles, 31, 33
traditional organization to business
community, 23–26
UBM company transition, 19–21,
26–30

competencies
behavior patterns, 16
and leadership for the Social Age,
15–16

competency development, 73–74

complexity
characteristics of, 155–156
cognitive, 162–164
as hallmark of Social Age, 155
versus linearity, 14, 155

confidence, 142

connected constituents
creating influence across constituents,
146
demand for authenticity, 147–148
emotional engagement, social
inclusion, and purpose, 139–140
leadership challenged unique to
Social Age, 9
and mass communication, 137–138
need for clarity, 143
need for emotional engagement, 144
need for purpose, 145–146
need for social inclusion, 144–145
and points of view, 138
Social Energy, 137

Index

Index

Index

mass communication, 137–138
mayors *versus* generals, 41
McCall, Morgan, 55, 79
meditation, 110
membership
  bureaucratic organization, 33
  business community adaptation, 33
  business community principle, 33
  community principles, 31
metaphors, 170–172
military heritage, 13
mindful development, 87–91
mindfulness
  behavior innovation, 88
  and CABs, 106–107
  developing tolerance for ambiguity, 161
  "internal theater" characteristic, 45–46
  peripheral awareness, 46, 105, 112–114
  productive and nonproductive CABs, 181
  remaining in the moment, 108–110
  self-awareness, 46, 105, 114–118
  situational awareness, 46, 105, 111–112
  social leadership assessment summary, 66
  social leadership personal themes, 64
  temporal awareness, 46, 104, 108–111
  as Tenet of Social Leadership, 16, 43
  of value preferences, 117
mindlessness, 108–109
mindset development, 80–81, 165
muscle memory concept, 76–77

N
needs
  to achieve, 114–115
  for affiliation, 114–115
  for clarity, 143
  for emotional engagement, 144, 147
  for power, 114, 116–117
  for purpose, 145–147
  for social inclusion, 144–145, 147
networked communities
  social leadership drivers, 7–8
Nokia company, 156–159, 163
nonjudgmental assessment
  tolerance of ambiguity, 40
novelty features (seminal situations), 78

O
openness
  adjusting perspective, 158–159
  behavior innovation, 88–89
  and cognitive complexity, 162–163
  "external leader" characteristic, 46–48
  to learning, 165
  to learning, growth, and ambiguity, 48
  productive and nonproductive CABs, 183–184
  social leadership assessment summary, 66
  social leadership personal themes, 64
  as Tenet of Social Leadership, 16, 44
opinion leadership, 31
ownership, affinity principles, 31

P
perception, others' stories of you, 149–150
performative artist, understanding and living your values, 128–129
performative contradiction, 128
peripheral awareness
  cultivating habit of curiosity, 113
  looking at adjacents to improve, 113–114
  and mindfulness, 105
  weak signals, 112–113
personal development, 32

Index

Index

situational awareness
  focusing on CABs to improve, 112
  and mindfulness, 105
  removing blinders to improve, 111
  suspending judgment to improve, 112
Smith, Patrick, 26
Social Age
  challenge of creating Social Energy
    in, 151
  and commercial Internet existence, 3
  communication principles, 177–179
  complexity as hallmark of, 155
  complexity *versus* linearity, 14
  defining features, 10
  digital technology forces, 6
  and discontinuity, 103–104
  driving forces, 10
  globalization forces, 6
  infrastructure, 95
  leadership challenges, 8–10
  and military heritage, 13
  mindset and attitude changes, 6
  rethinking leadership for, 14–16
  Social Energy as key resource of, 37–38
  social leadership characteristics, 7–8
  staying relevant in, 11–13
  and top down management struggle,
    3–5
Social Energy
  calmness, 142
  core organizational challenge and, 25
  creating influence across constituents,
    146
  emotion, 151
  harnessing to focus on common
    goals, 138
  as key resource of Social Age, 37–38
  need for clarity, 143
  need for emotional engagement, 144,
    147
  need for purpose, 145–147
  need for social inclusion, 144–145, 147

  outward-seeking behavior, 142
  power to harness, 151
  purpose as factor in generating, 162
  sense of confidence, 142
  shift of focus to client retention, 146
  upward and downward spirals,
    140–142, 146–147
social inclusion
  CABs focused on, 147
  need for, 144–145, 147
social information
  connected constituents challenge, 137
  leadership challenges unique to
    Social Age, 9–10
Social Leader
  defined, 7
  field of action, 39–40
social leadership. *See also* leadership
  assessment summary, 66–67
  personal themes, 64
  self-interview, 68
  Social Age characteristics, 7–8
  Tenets of Social Leadership, 16–17
social leadership development
  and behavior patterns, 76–77
  and CABs, 72, 77
  competency development, 73–74
  "learn-then do" approach, 75–77
  "learn-while doing" approach, 77
  mindful development, 87–91
  mindset development, 80–81
  purposeful intent, 82
  reconciling the learning impact, 75
  self-awareness, 81, 85–87
  seminal experiences in application,
    83–87
  and seminal situations, 78–79
  technical *versus* adaptive approaches,
    73–74
  thought-full seminal development,
    80–82
  thought-less seminal experience, 79

Index

About the Authors

Frank Guglielmo, Ph.D., Managing Director of Park Consulting, is an award-winning educator, consultant, and coach. He has created and led executive development programs around the world for over two decades and coached executives in a wide range of industries.

Prior to founding Park Consulting, Frank held executive positions in a number of Fortune 500 companies including Interpublic Group, Altria Group, and Prudential Securities; and has consulted in industries ranging from media and advertising, FMCG, financial services, bio-tech and telecommunications. His work in leadership development has included working with C-suite executives and boards on talent assessment, succession planning, and high potential executive development.

Sudhanshu Palsule is an award-winning educator, and regarded as one of the leading thinkers in the field of Transformative Leadership. He works globally as a leadership professor, CEO advisor and consultant to several Fortune 500 organizations and to the United Nations. He teaches at Duke CE and in the Advanced Management Program at INSEAD.

Palsule's work in transformative leadership is a unique combination of the latest research in psychology and neurology and his own exploration of the human mind for the past three decades. Trained as a physicist, he uses principles of Quantum Physics to help senior executives negotiate complexity by helping them develop their mindfulness. Palsule has written several books including *Science, Technology, and Social Change*, *Managing in Four Worlds*, *The Ecology of Organizations*, and *Personal Growth*.